The Morality of Capitalism

What Your Professors Won't Tell You

Edited by Tom G. Palmer
Students For Liberty & Atlas Network

JAMESON BOOKS, INC.
Ottawa, Illinois

AtlasNetwork.org   StudentsForLiberty.org

"The Market Economy and the Distribution of Wealth," by Ludwig Lachmann reprinted by permission of the Institute for Humane Studies. "Human Betterment through Globalization," by Vernon Smith reprinted by permission of the Foundation for Economic Education. All other essays published by permission of the authors.

Edited by Tom G. Palmer
Cover Design by Jon Meyers

The editor gratefully acknowledges the assistance in preparing this book, not only of the authors and copyright holders, but of the members of Students For Liberty, most especially Clark Ruper, Brandon Wasicsko, and Ankur Chawla, who worked tirelessly to format and prepare the essays for publication. Their dedication and zeal for liberty is itself an inspiration.

For information and other requests please write

Students For Liberty
P.O. Box 17321
Arlington, VA 22216

Jameson Books, Inc.
722 Columbus Street
P.O. Box 738
Ottawa, IL 61350
800-426-1357

Jameson Books are distributed to the book trade by Midpoint Trade Books, New York

ISBN: 978-0-89803-170-6

Printed in the United States of America

15 14 13 12 11 5 4 3 2 1

Contents

Section III: The Production and Distribution of Wealth

Section IV: Globalizing Capitalism

Introduction: The Morality of Capitalism

By Tom G. Palmer

This book is about the moral justification of what philosopher Robert Nozick called "capitalist acts among consenting adults."[1] It's about the system of cooperative production and free exchange characterized by the predominance of such acts.

A few words about the title—*The Morality of Capitalism*—are in order. The essays in this book are about the *morality* of capitalism; they are not confined to abstract moral philosophy, but also draw on economics, logic, history, literature, and other disciplines. Moreover, they are about the morality of *capitalism*, not merely the morality of free exchange. The term "capitalism" refers not just to markets for the exchange of goods and services, which have existed since time immemorial, but to the system of innovation, wealth creation, and social change that has brought to billions of people prosperity that was unimaginable to earlier generations of human beings.

Capitalism refers to a legal, social, economic, and cultural system that embraces equality of rights and "careers open to talent" and that energizes decentralized innovation and processes of trial and error—what the economist Joseph Schumpeter called "creative destruction"—through the voluntary processes of market exchange. Capitalist culture celebrates the entrepreneur, the scientist, the risk-taker, the innovator, the creator. Although derided as materialistic by philosophers (notably Marxists) who are themselves adherents of materialism, capitalism is at its core a spiritual and cultural enterprise. As the historian Joyce Appleby noted in her recent study *The Relentless Revolution: A History of Capitalism*, "Because capitalism is a cultural system and not simply an economic one, it cannot be explained by material factors alone."[2]

Capitalism is a system of cultural, spiritual, and ethical values. As the economists David Schwab and Elinor Ostrom noted in a seminal game-theoretic study of the role of norms and rules in maintaining open economies, free markets rest firmly on the norms that constrain us from stealing and that are "trust enhancing."[3] Far from being an amoral arena for the clash of interests, as capitalism is often portrayed by those who seek to undermine or destroy it, capitalist interaction is highly structured by ethical norms and rules. Indeed, capitalism rests on a rejection of the ethics of loot and grab, the means by which most wealth enjoyed by the wealthy has been acquired in other economic and political systems. (In fact, in many countries today, and for much of human history, it has been widely understood that those who are rich are rich because they took from others, and especially because they have access to organized force—in today's terms, the state. Such predatory elites use this force to gain monopolies and to confiscate the produce of others through taxes. They feed at the state treasury and they benefit from state-imposed monopolies and restrictions on competition. It's only under conditions of capitalism that people commonly become wealthy without being criminals.)

Consider what the economist and historian Deirdre McCloskey calls *"The Great Fact":* "Real income per head nowadays exceeds that around 1700 or 1800 in, say, Britain and other countries that have experienced modern economic growth by such a large factor as sixteen, at least."[4] That is unprecedented in all of human history. McCloskey's estimate is, in fact, quite conservative. It doesn't take into effect the amazing advances in science and technology that have put the cultures of the world at our fingertips.

Capitalism puts human creativity to the service of humanity by respecting and encouraging entrepreneurial innovation, that elusive factor that explains the difference between the way we live now and how generation after generation after generation of our ancestors lived prior to the nineteenth century. The innovations that have transformed human life for the better are not merely scientific and technological, but institutional, as well. New business firms of all kinds voluntarily coordinate the work efforts of enormous numbers of people. New financial markets and instruments connect the savings and investment decisions of billions of people twenty-four hours a day. New telecommunications networks bring together people from the corners of the world. (Today I had conversations with friends in Finland,

China, Morocco, the United States, and Russia, and Facebook comments and communications from friends and acquaintances in the United States, Canada, Pakistan, Denmark, France, and Kyrgyzstan.) New products offer us opportunities for comfort, delight, and education unimaginable to previous generations. (I am writing this on my Apple MacBook Pro.) Those changes have made our societies in countless ways dramatically unlike all human societies that have preceded them.

Capitalism is not just about building stuff, in the way that socialist dictators used to exhort their slaves to "Build the Future!" Capitalism is about creating value, not merely working hard or making sacrifices or being busy. Those who fail to understand capitalism are quick to support "job creation" programs to create work. They have misunderstood the point of work, much less the point of capitalism. In a much-quoted story, the economist Milton Friedman was shown the construction on a massive new canal in Asia. When he noted that it was odd that the workers were moving huge amounts of earth and rock with small shovels, rather than earth moving equipment, he was told "You don't understand; this is a jobs program." His response: "Oh, I thought you were trying to build a canal. If you're seeking to create jobs, why didn't you issue them spoons, rather than shovels?"

The mercantilist and cronyist H. Ross Perot, when running for president of the United States in 1992, lamented during the presidential debates that Americans were buying computer chips from Taiwan and selling the Taiwanese potato chips. It seemed that Perot was ashamed that Americans were selling mere potato chips; he had bought into Lenin's view that value is added only by industrial production in factories. Economist Michael Boskin of Stanford University correctly noted that if you're talking about a dollar's worth of computer chips, or a dollar's worth of potato chips, you're talking about a dollar's worth. Adding value by growing potatoes in Idaho or by etching silicon in Taipei is adding value. Comparative advantage[5] is a key to specialization and trade; there is nothing degrading about producing value, as a farmer, as a furniture mover (I worked with three movers today to move much of my library and I have a very solid sense of how much value they added to my life), as a financier, and so on. The market—not arrogant mercantilist politicians—shows us when we are adding value, and without free markets, we cannot know.

Capitalism is not just about people trading butter for eggs in local markets, which has gone on for millennia. It's about adding value through the mobilization of human energy and ingenuity on a scale never seen before in human history, to create wealth for common people that would have dazzled and astonished the richest and most powerful kings, sultans, and emperors of the past. It's about the erosion of long-entrenched systems of power, domination, and privilege, and the opening of "careers to talent." It's about the replacement of force by persuasion.[6] It's about the replacement of envy by accomplishment.[7] It's about what has made my life possible, and yours.

(The only thing that the kings and sultans and emperors had that ordinary people today don't have was power over other people and the ability to command them. They had vast palaces built by slaves or financed by taxes, but no indoor heating or cooling; slaves and servants, but no washing machines or dishwashers; armies of couriers, but no cell phones or Wi-Fi; court doctors and magi, but no anesthetic to ease their agony or antibiotics to cure infections; they were powerful, but they were miserably poor by our standards.)

The History of a Word

Free markets, understood as systems of free exchange among persons with well-defined, legally secure, and transferable rights in scarce resources, are a necessary condition for the wealth of the modern world. But as economic historians, most notably Deirdre McCloskey, have convincingly shown, they are not sufficient. Something else is needed: an ethics of free exchange and of wealth production through innovation.

A few words about the use of the term "capitalism" are in order. The social historian Fernand Braudel traced the term "capital" to the period spanning the twelfth and thirteenth centuries, when it referred to "funds, stock of merchandise, sum of money, or money carrying interest."[8] Of the many uses of the term "capitalist" that Braudel catalogued, he noted dryly, "The word is never . . . used in a friendly sense."[9] The word "Capitalism" emerged as a term, generally of abuse, in the nineteenth century, e.g., when the French socialist Louis Blanc defined the term as "the appropriation of capital by some to the exclusion of others."[10] Karl Marx used the term "capitalist mode of production," and it was his ardent follower Werner Sombart who popularized the term "capitalism" in his influential 1912 book *Der Moderne Kapitalismus*. (Marx's collaborator, Friedrich Engels, considered Sombart the only thinker in Germany who really understood Marx; Sombart later became a cheerleader for another form of anti-capitalism, National Socialism, i.e., Nazism.)

In their attack on the "capitalists" and the "capitalist mode of production," Marx and Engels noted that "the bourgeoisie" (his term for the "class" who owned "the means of production") had radically changed the world:

> The bourgeoisie, during its rule of scarce one hundred years, has created more massive and more colossal productive forces than have all preceding generations together. Subjection of Nature's forces to man, machinery, application of chemistry to industry and agriculture, steam-navigation, railways, electric telegraphs, clearing of whole continents for cultivation, canalisation of rivers, whole populations conjured out of the ground—what earlier century had even a presentiment that such productive forces slumbered in the lap of social labour?[11]

Marx and Engels marveled at not only technological innovation, but at "whole populations conjured out of the ground," which is a striking way to describe falling death rates, rising living standards, and increasing life spans. Despite such accomplishments, of course, Marx and Engels called for the destruction of the "capitalist mode of production," or, to be more precise, they thought that it would destroy itself and usher in a new system that would be so wonderful that it was not necessary—indeed, it was even offensively unscientific—to offer even the slightest hint as to how it might work.[12]

More importantly, Marx and Engels grounded their critique of capitalism (a critique that, despite the failure of all communist orders to fulfill their promises, remains extraordinarily influential among intellectuals around the world) on a mass of confusion over what they meant by the term "bourgeoisie," which they connected to the "capitalist mode of production." On the one hand, they use the term to mean owners of "capital" who organize productive enterprises, but on the other they use it to refer to those who live off of the state and its power, as Marx did in one of his most interesting essays on politics:

> [T]he material interest of the French bourgeoisie is most intimately imbricated [Note: a term for "overlapping"] precisely with the maintenance of that extensive and highly ramified state machine. It is that machine which provides its surplus population with jobs, and makes up through state salaries for what it cannot pocket in the form of profits, interest, rents, and fees. Its political interest equally compelled it daily to increase the repression, and therefore to increase the resources and the personnel of the state power.[13]

So on the one hand, Marx identified the "bourgeoisie" with the entrepreneurs who gave "a cosmopolitan character to production and consumption in every country," who made "national one-sidedness and narrow-mindedness" "more and more impossible," who created "a world literature," who brought about "the rapid improvement of all instruments of production" and "immensely facilitated the means of communication," and who overcame "the barbarians' obstinate hatred of foreigners" by the "cheap prices of commodities" they offered.[14] On the other, he used "bourgeoisie" to refer to those who live off of "public credit" (i.e., government debt):

> The whole of the modern money market, the whole of the banking business, is most intimately interwoven with public credit. A part of their business capital is necessarily put out at interest in short-term public funds. Their deposits, the capital put at their disposal by merchants and industrialists and distributed by them among the same people, flow in part from the dividends of holders of government bonds.[15]

Marx saw the "bourgeoisie" as intimately involved in and benefiting from the struggle to control the machinery of the state:

> All political upheavals perfected this machine instead of smashing it. The parties that strove in turn for mastery regarded possession of this immense state edifice as the main booty for the victory.[16]

In the words of the historian Shirley Gruner, "Marx felt he had got a grip on reality when he found the 'bourgeoisie' but in fact he had merely got hold of a very slippery term."[17] In some texts Marx used the term to refer to those innovative entrepreneurs who organize productive enterprises and invest in wealth creation, and in others he used it to refer to those who cluster around the state, who live off of taxation, who lobby to prohibit competition and restrict the freedom to trade; in brief, to those who invest, not in creating wealth, but in securing the power to redistribute or destroy the wealth of others, and to keep markets closed, the poor in their place, and society under their thumbs.

Because of the influence of Marx and his follower Sombart, the term "capitalism" came into general use. It's worth remembering that the term was popularized by people who not only confused productive entrepreneurship and market exchange with living off of taxes taken from others, but who advocated the abolition of property, markets, money, prices, the division of labor, and the entire edifice of liberalism: individual rights, religious freedom, freedom of speech, equality before the law, and constitutionally limited democratic government.

Not uncommonly, like many terms of abuse, "capitalism" was taken up by some of those intellectual advocates of free markets against whom the term was wielded. As a result of its history, those who adopted the term "capitalism" for what they advocated, or even simply as a neutral term for social scientific discussion, were disadvantaged by the facts that (1) the term was used equivocally (to refer to both free market entrepreneurship and to living off taxes and government power and patronage), and (2) that it was almost always used in a distinctly negative manner.

Some suggest abandoning the term altogether, because it is so fraught with conflicting meanings and ideological overtones.[18] That's tempting, but there remains a problem. Merely allowing people to trade freely and to be guided by profits and losses, while certainly necessary for economic progress, is not sufficient for the creation of the modern world. Modern markets both emerged from and fuel a whirlwind of institutional, technological, cultural, artistic, and social innovation that transcends the model of people exchanging eggs for butter. Modern free-market capitalism innovates, not at a glacial pace over millennia, but faster and faster—precisely what both the socialists (notably Marx) and their allies, the anti-market conservatives, found so terrifying about the modern world. In his *Capitalism, Socialism, and Democracy*, Joseph Schumpeter criticized those for whom "the problem that is usually being visualized is how capitalism administers existing structures, whereas the relevant problem is how it creates and destroys them."[19]

Modern free markets are not merely places of exchange, as were the market fairs of old. They are characterized by waves of "creative destruction"; what was new ten years ago is already old, superseded by improved versions, by new devices, institutional arrangements, technologies, and ways of interacting that were unimagined by anyone. That is what distinguishes modern free markets from the markets of old. The best available term to distinguish the free-market relations that have made the modern world from those markets that preceded it, in my opinion, is "capitalism."

Capitalism isn't a form of disorder, though. It's a form of spontaneous order, which emerges from a process. (Some writers refer to such orders as "emergent orders.") The predictable constancy of the rule of law and security of rights make possible such innovation. As David Boaz noted in *The Futurist*,

People have always had trouble seeing the order in an apparently chaotic market. Even as the price system constantly moves resources toward their best use, on the surface the market seems the very opposite of order—businesses failing, jobs being lost, people prospering at an uneven pace, investments revealed to have been wasted. The fast-paced Innovation Age will seem even more chaotic, with huge businesses rising and falling more rapidly than ever, and fewer people having long-term jobs. But the increased efficiency of transportation, communications, and capital markets will in fact mean even more order than the market could achieve in the industrial age. The point is to avoid using coercive government to "smooth out the excesses" or "channel" the market toward someone's desired result.[20]

Free-Market Capitalism vs. Crony Capitalism

In order to avoid the confusion caused by equivocal use of the term "capitalism" by socialist intellectuals, "free-market capitalism" should be clearly distinguished from "crony capitalism," from the system that has mired so many nations in corruption and backwardness. In many countries, if someone is rich, there is a very good chance that he (rarely she) holds political power or is a close relative, friend, or supporter—in a word, a "crony"—of those who do hold power, and that that person's wealth came, not from being a producer of valued goods, but from enjoying the privileges that the state can confer on some at the expense of others. Sadly, "crony capitalism" is a term that can with increasing accuracy also be applied to the economy of the United States, a country in which failed firms are routinely "bailed out" with money taken from taxpayers, in which the national capital is little more than a gigantic pulsating hive of "rent-seeking" lobbyists, bureaucrats, politicians, consultants, and hacks, and in which appointed officials of the Treasury Department and the central bank (the Federal Reserve System) take it on themselves to reward some firms and harm others. Such corrupt cronyism shouldn't be confused with "free-market capitalism," which refers to a system of production and exchange that is based on the rule of law, on equality of rights for all, on the freedom to choose, on the freedom to trade, on the freedom to innovate, on the guiding discipline of profits and losses, and on the right to enjoy the fruits of one's labors, of one's savings, of one's investments, without fearing confiscation or restriction from those who have invested, not in production of wealth, but in political power.

The waves of change that free-market capitalism creates are

often resented by entrenched elites. As they see the world, minorities become uppity and the lower classes no longer know their place. More shocking, from their perspective, is that under free-market capitalism women assert their own worth. Status is undermined. People create relationships based on choice and consent, rather than birth or status.[21] The conservative hatred of free-market capitalism, which was very neatly summarized and incorporated by Marx into his writings, reflects anger at such change and often anger at the loss of privilege. Leo Melamed (the Chairman Emeritus of the CME Group [formerly the Chicago Mercantile Exchange] whose own life story of escaping from the Gestapo and the KGB and going on to revolutionize world finance is a story of courage and vision), drew on his experience when he said that "in Chicago's financial markets it is not what you are—your personal pedigree, your family origin, your physical infirmities, your gender—but your ability to determine what the customer wants and where the market is headed. Little else matters."[22] Embracing free-market capitalism means embracing the freedom to change, to innovate, to invent. It means accommodating change and respecting the freedom of others to do as they please with what is theirs. It means making place for new technologies, new scientific theories, new forms of art, and new identities and new relationships. It means embracing the freedom to create wealth, which is the only means to the elimination of poverty. (Wealth has causes, but poverty does not; poverty is what results if wealth production does not take place, whereas wealth is not what results if poverty production does not take place.)[23] It means celebrating human liberation and realizing human potential.

The authors whose essays are presented here come from a variety of countries and cultures and from a variety of callings and intellectual disciplines. Each offers an appreciation of how free-market exchanges are rooted in morality and reinforce moral behavior. The selection includes a mix of essays, some quite short, some longer, some quite accessible, some more academic. It includes two essays that have not previously appeared in English and were translated from Chinese and Russian for this collection. It includes contributions by two Nobel Prize winners, one a novelist and one an economist, and an interview with a successful entrepreneur who is an outspoken proponent of what he calls "conscious capitalism." The essays don't provide all of the arguments for free-market capitalism, but they do provide an introduction to a very rich literature. (A small sample of that literature is listed in the brief bibliography at the end of the book.)

Why does this book only contain vigorous defenses of free-market capitalism? Because there are hundreds—actually, thousands—of books on the market purporting to offer "balanced" discussions that in fact are filled with nothing but indictments of wealth creation, of entrepreneurship, of innovation, of the profit-and-loss system, and of free-market capitalism generally. In the course of my own career, I have read hundreds of books that attacked free-market capitalism; I've thought about the arguments and wrestled with them. In contrast, it is unusual to find critics of free-market capitalism who have read more than one author who dared to offer a defense of free-market capitalism. The one author who is most commonly cited, at least in the modern Anglo-Saxon intellectual world, is Robert Nozick, and even then it becomes clear that only one chapter of one book was read, the one in which he offered a challenging hypothetical thought experiment to test enemies of free-market capitalism. Most socialists think it sufficient to read one essay and rebut one thought experiment.[24] After reading and rebutting one argument, if those who condemn free-market capitalism even think it worthwhile to continue the critique, they usually rely on one or another misstatement or garbled version of what Milton Friedman or Ayn Rand or F. A. Hayek or Adam Smith believed, offered without citation.

To take one recent prominent example, Harvard professor Michael Sandel offered a rebuttal to the case for free-market capitalism in his recent book *Justice: What's the Right Thing to Do?*; besides Nozick, he cited Friedman and Hayek, but made it clear that he had not read them. He quoted Friedman asking, "Are we entitled to use coercion to prevent him [someone who won't save for retirement] from doing what he chooses to do?"[25] But he failed to note that in the very next paragraph Friedman actually offered reasons for such coercion[26] and stated that "The weight of this argument clearly depends on fact."[27] (Friedman was invoking the classical liberal principle of the "presumption of liberty,"[28] not making a categorical statement about rights, as Sandel incorrectly claims.) Sandel also states that "In *The Constitution of Liberty* (1960), the Austrian-born economist-philosopher Friedrich A. Hayek (1899-1992) argued that 'any attempt to bring about greater economic equality was bound to be coercive and destructive of a free society'"—a claim that Hayek does not, in fact, make; he does argue that "progressive income taxation" (in which the rates of tax increase with income) is incompatible with the rule of law, for "unlike proportionality, progression provides no principle which tells us what the relative burden of different persons ought to be,"[29] but that is not the same as arguing that any attempt to bring about greater economic equality (say, by eliminating special subsidies and privileges for the rich) was bound to be coercive. (Both Sandel's erroneous claim and his description show that Sandel didn't even bother to consult Hayek's book; one wonders whether he would have described Adam Smith's *An Inquiry into the Nature and Causes of the Wealth of Nations* as a book about how pins are manufactured.)

Serious people should do better. I strongly encourage you, the reader of this essay and this book, to do better. Read the best criticisms of free-market capitalism. Read Marx. Read Sombart. Read Rawls. Read Sandel. Understand them. Be open to being convinced by them. Think about them. I've read more arguments against free-market capitalism than most enemies of free-market capitalism have read, and I think I could usually make their case better than they can, because I know it better. What's offered here is the other side of the debate, the side that is rarely even acknowledged to exist.

So, go ahead, take a chance. Wrestle with the arguments offered by the essays in this book. Think about them. Then make up your own mind.

—Tom G. Palmer
Washington, D.C.

Section I

The Virtues of
Entrepreneurial Capitalism

Interview with an Entrepreneur

Featuring John Mackey

Conducted by Tom G. Palmer

In this interview, business entrepreneur and Whole Foods Co-Founder and Co-CEO John Mackey explains his philosophy of "conscious capitalism" and shares his thoughts on human nature and motivation, the nature of business, and the distinction between free-market capitalism and "crony capitalism."

John Mackey co-founded Whole Foods Market in 1980. He has been a leader in promoting healthy eating, ethical treatment of animals, and positive community involvement by businesses. He is a trustee of the Conscious Capitalism Institute.

Palmer: John, you're something of a rarity in the business world: an entrepreneur who's unashamed to defend the morality of capitalism. You're also known for saying that self-interest isn't enough for capitalism. What do you mean by that?

Mackey: Resting everything on self-interest is relying on a very incomplete theory of human nature. It reminds me of college debates with people who tried to argue that everything you do logically has to come from self-interest or you wouldn't do it. That position is irrefutable, and ultimately nonsense, since even if you did things that weren't in your self-interest, they would *still* say that it was in your self-interest or you wouldn't do it. So it's a circular argument.

Palmer: In what way do you think that other motivations beyond self-interest are important for capitalism?

Mackey: I just don't like the question, because people have different definitions of self-interest and you end up talking past each other frequently when you talk about this subject, which is why I was mentioning the sophomoric type of discussion you have in college about everything being self-interest. What I'm suggesting is that human beings are complex and we have many motivations, of which self-interest is one, but hardly the only one. We're motivated by many things that we care about, that include, but are not limited to, our self-interest. I think that in some ways the libertarian movement—possibly due to the combined influence of Ayn Rand and many economists—has gotten to a kind of ideological dead end that I don't think does justice to business or capitalism or human nature.

If you think about it, the time in our lives when we're probably the most self-interested is when we're young and emotionally immature. Most children and adolescents are highly self-involved or narcissistic. They're acting from their self-interest, as they perceive it. As we mature and we grow, we become more capable of empathy and compassion and love and a fuller range of human emotions. People do things for lots of reasons. A false dichotomy is often set up between self-interest, or selfishness, and altruism. To me it is a false dichotomy, because we're obviously both. We are self-interested, but we're not *just* self-interested. We also care about other people. We usually care a great deal about the well-being of our families. We usually care about our communities and the larger society that we live in. We can also care about the well-being of animals and our larger environment. We have ideals that motivate us to try to make the world a better place. By a strict definition, they would seem to contradict self-interest, unless you get back into the circular argument that everything you care about and want to do is self-interest.

So I don't think self-interest is enough. I don't think calling every act self-interested is a good theory of human nature. I think that capitalism and business should fully reflect the complexity of human nature. I also think it does great damage to the "brands" of business and capitalism, because it allows the enemies of capitalism and business to portray them as selfish and greedy and exploitative. That really bothers me, Tom, because capitalism and business are the greatest forces for good in the world. It's been that way for at least the last three hundred years . . . and they don't get sufficient credit for the amazing value that they have created.

Palmer: What, besides pursuing self-interest, or profit, does a business do?

Mackey: Putting it generally, successful businesses create value. The beautiful thing about capitalism is that it's ultimately based on voluntary exchange for mutual benefit. Take a business like Whole Foods Market, for example: we create value for our customers through the goods and services we provide for them. They don't *have* to trade with us; they do it because they want to, because they think it's in their interest to do so. So we're creating value for them. We create value for the people that work for us: our team members. None of them are slaves. They are all voluntarily working because they feel like it's a job they want to do; the pay is satisfactory; they derive many benefits from working at Whole Foods, psychic as well as monetary. So we're creating value for them. We're creating value for our investors, because, well, our market cap's over $10 billion dollars and we started at nothing! So we've created over $10 billion dollars' worth of value for our investors over the past thirty-plus years. None of our stockholders are forced to own our stock. They all do so voluntarily because they believe we're creating value for them. We're creating value for our suppliers, who trade with our business. I've watched them over the years, watched their businesses grow, watched them flourish—and that's all proceeded voluntarily. They help make Whole Foods better and we help make them better.

Palmer: You label your philosophy "conscious capitalism." What do you mean by that?

Mackey: We use that term to distinguish it from all those other labels that generate a lot of confusion when they're all lumped together, like "corporate social responsibility," or Bill Gates's "creative capitalism," or "sustainable capitalism." We have a very clear definition of conscious capitalism, based on four principles.

The first principle is that business has the potential to have a higher purpose that may include making money, but is not restricted to it. So every business has the potential for a higher purpose. And if you think about it, all the other professions in our society are motivated by purpose, beyond a narrow interpretation of purpose as restricted to maximizing profits. Doctors are some of the highest paid people in our society and yet doctors have a purpose—to heal people—and that's the professional ethics taught in medical school. That's not to say that there are no greedy doctors out there, but at least many of the doctors I've known do genuinely care about their patients and try to heal them when they're sick. Teachers try to educate people and architects design buildings and lawyers—once you've taken all the lawyer jokes out of the equation—are attempting to promote justice and fairness in our society. Every profession has a purpose beyond maximizing profits and so does business. Whole Foods is a grocer, so we're selling high-quality natural and organic foods for people and helping them to live healthier and longer lives.

Palmer: And the second principle?

Mackey: The second principle of conscious capitalism is the stakeholder principle, which I alluded to earlier, which is that you should think about the different stakeholders for which a business creates value and who can impact a business. You should think about the complexity of your business in the attempt to create value for all of these interdependent stakeholders—customers, employees, suppliers, investors, and communities.

The third principle is that a business needs leaders who are highly ethical and who put the purpose of the business first. They attempt to serve that purpose and they attempt to follow the stakeholder principle. So they have to walk the talk of the business.

And the fourth principle of conscious capitalism is that you have to create a culture that supports purpose, stakeholders, and leadership, so that it all fits together.

Palmer: Do those principles motivate you personally when you get up in the morning? Do you say, "I'm going to make another dollar" or "I'm going to be true to my core principles"?

Mackey: I guess I'm a little bit odd in this respect, because I haven't taken any salary from Whole Foods for almost five years now. Or bonuses. The stock options, which I would be entitled to, are given to The Whole Planet Foundation to make micro-credit loans to poor people around the world. I'm highly motivated by the purpose of Whole Foods, rather than by how much money I could potentially extract from the business in terms of compensation. I believe that I personally have more than enough wealth from the stock that I still own in the company.

Palmer: And, once again, how do you define that purpose?

Mackey: The purpose of Whole Foods is ... well, if we had more time, we could talk at some length about the higher purpose of Whole Foods. I gave a talk to our Leadership Group about two weeks ago. What I can say in about a minute is that our company is organized around seven core values. Our first core value is to satisfy and delight our customers. Our second core value is team member happiness and excellence. (This is all on our website, by the way, so we make it quite public.) Our third core value is creating wealth through profits and growth. The fourth core value is being good citizens in the communities where we do business. The fifth core value is to try to do our business with environmental integrity. The sixth core value is that we view our suppliers as partners and we try to engage in win-win relationships with them. And seventh we wish to educate all of our stakeholders about healthy lifestyle and healthy eating. So our higher purposes are a direct extension of those core values. Some of these include: trying to heal America; our nation's fat and sick and we eat terrible diets and we die of heart disease and cancer and diabetes. Those are lifestyle diseases—those are largely avoidable or reversible diseases, so that's one of our higher purposes. We have a higher purpose about our agricultural system, to try to make it a more sustainable agricultural system that also has a high degree of productivity.

The third higher purpose is connected to our Whole Planet Foundation, working with Grameen Trust and other micro-credit organizations [Editor's Note: Grameen Bank and Grameen Trust promote microfinance in poor countries, especially for women, as a path to development.] to try to help end poverty across the planet. We're now in 34 countries—it will be 56 in two years—and that's having a positive impact on hundreds of thousands of people already. Our fourth higher purpose is the spread of conscious capitalism.

Palmer: You've talked about the purposes of a business, so . . . why have profits? Isn't a business a profit-maximizing enterprise? Couldn't you do all of this without having any profits? Couldn't you just make enough money to cover your costs?

Mackey: One answer is that you wouldn't be very effective, because if you're only making enough money to cover your costs, then your impact's going to be very limited. Whole Foods has a much greater impact today than we had thirty, or twenty, or fifteen, or ten years ago. Because we've been highly profitable, because we've been able to grow and to realize our purposes more and more, we've been able to reach and help millions of people instead of just a few thousand people. So I think profit is essential in order to better fulfill your purpose. Also, creating profits provides the capital that our world needs to innovate and progress—no profits, then no progress. They are completely interdependent.

Palmer: But if the profits are going into the pockets of your shareholders, then is it fulfilling the mission as much as it could?

Mackey: Of course most of our profits don't go into the pockets of our shareholders. Only the relatively small percentage that we pay out in dividends does. Ninety-plus percent of the money we have made has been reinvested in the business for growth. Strictly speaking, if we paid out one hundred percent of our profits as dividends then that would be true, but I don't know of any business that does that other than a REIT, a Real Estate Investment Trust. Everybody else reinvests for growth. Moreover, profit for shareholders induces them to invest in the business in the first place, without which you'd have no capital at all to realize your higher purposes. The ability to increase the capital value of a firm means you're able to create value, and a good measure of that is your share price. That's what I meant when I said that we had created over $10 billion dollars' worth of value over the past thirty-plus years.

Palmer: People sometimes say that free markets create inequality. What do you think of that claim?

Mackey: I don't think it is true. Extreme poverty has been the normal human condition for most people throughout all of history. Human beings were all equally poor and lived fairly short lives. Two hundred years ago 85 percent of the people alive on the planet earth lived on less than a dollar a day in today's dollars—85 percent! That figure's down to only 20 percent now and by the end of this century it should be virtually zero. So it's a rising tide. The world is becoming richer. People are moving out of poverty. Humanity really *is* advancing. Our culture is advancing. Our intelligence is advancing. We are on an upward spiral, if we manage not to destroy ourselves, which is of course a risk, because people can be warlike at times, too. And that, by the way, is one of the reasons we should work to promote business and enterprise and wealth creation, as a healthier outlet for energy than militarism, political conflict, and wealth destruction. But that's another big topic.

So does that increase inequality? I suppose it's not so much that capitalism creates inequality, as it helps people to become more prosperous, and inevitably that means that not everybody is going to rise at the same rate, but everybody ultimately rises over time. We've seen that happen, particularly in the past twenty years as we've seen literally hundreds of millions of people lifted out of poverty in China and India as they have embraced more capitalism. The reality is that some people are simply escaping poverty and becoming prosperous sooner than other people are. Now that's not *causing* poverty—it is ending poverty. It's not causing inequality in the way most people think of the term. There's always been inequality in any type of social organization throughout history. Even communism, which purported to produce a society of equal ownership of wealth, was highly stratified and had elites who had special privileges. So I don't see that inequality should be blamed on capitalism. Capitalism enables people to escape from poverty and become more prosperous and wealthy and that is very good. That's the issue that we should focus on.

The big gap in the world is between those countries that have adopted free-market capitalism, and became rich, and those that haven't, and stayed poor. The problem is not that some became rich, but that others stayed poor. And that doesn't have to be!

Palmer: You've distinguished free-market capitalism from other systems in which people also make profits and have businesses, but which are often characterized as "crony capitalism." What's the difference between your moral vision and what exists in a lot of countries around the world?

Mackey: You've got to have the rule of law. People have to have rules that apply equally to everyone, and those have to be enforced by a justice system that has that goal in the forefront of their consciousness. We need an equal application of the law to everyone as the primary goal—no special privileges to some and not to others. So what's happening in a lot of societies, and what I think is happening more and more in America, is you've got special favors given to the people who have political connections. It's wrong. It's bad. To the degree that any society suffers from crony capitalism, or what my friend Michael Strong calls "crapitalism," you are not in a free-market society any longer and you're not optimizing prosperity; you're unnecessarily keeping many, many people less prosperous than they would be if you had a truly free-market order with the rule of law supporting it.

Palmer: Let's turn to the country you live in, the United States. Do you think that there's any cronyism in the U.S.?

Mackey: Let me give my favorite current example. Well, I've got two. One is that we now have well over a thousand waivers that have already been granted by the Obama Administration for their rules and regulations that were passed under Obamacare.

That's a form of crony capitalism. The rules are not being applied equally to everyone. And that means that the power to give a waiver also means the power to deny one. And you can deny it to those who aren't making the proper donations to the political party in power or who you just, for whatever reason, you don't favor. You have an arbitrary law that you can selectively apply to some and not to others.

Second, I see crony capitalism right now in all of these subsidies that are going into "green technology," for example. They're subsidizing some businesses and, ultimately, since the government doesn't have any money on its own, it's taking it from taxpayers and redistributing it to people who are politically favored. I see what's happening with General Electric now, in terms of the kind of taxes they're paying, with all the special exemptions and deductions that get written into the tax laws. And since they're so heavily into these alternative energy technologies, or some of them, they're getting to a point where they do not have to pay taxes on most of their income, just because they're politically connected. So it offends me. I think it's a very bad thing.

Palmer: Would you call it immoral?

Mackey: Yes, I would. Immoral . . . well, *I* call it immoral. But then you get to the point of having to define what that means. It certainly violates my ethics and my sense of right and wrong. Whether that violates other people's ethics or not, it's hard to say. I certainly don't like it. I'm opposed to it. It's not compatible with my idea of how society should be governed. That sort of thing shouldn't happen in a society that has a strong rule of law.

Palmer: Who do you see as the main gainers from the free-market capitalism that you embrace?

Mackey: Everyone! Everyone in society is a beneficiary. It is what has lifted much of humanity out of poverty. It's what made this country wealthy. We were dirt poor. America was a land of opportunity, but it was not a wealthy country. Even though America surely hasn't been perfect, it's enjoyed one of the freest markets in the world for a couple of hundred years, and as a result we've grown from very poor to a prosperous, authentically rich country.

Palmer: In her book *Bourgeois Dignity*, Deirdre McCloskey argued that it was a change in the way that people thought about business and entrepreneurial innovation that made possible prosperity for the common person. Do you think that we can recapture that respect for wealth-creating businesses again?

Mackey: I think we can, because I saw what happened when Ronald Reagan got elected. America was in decline in the 1970s—there's no doubt about it; look at where our inflation was, where interest rates were, where GDP was heading, the frequency of recessions, we were suffering from "stagflation" that revealed the deep flaws of Keynesian philosophy, and then we had a leader who came in and cut taxes and freed up a lot of industries through deregulation and America experienced a renaissance, a rebirth, and that pretty much carried us for the past twenty-five years or more. We had basically an upward spiral of growth and progress. Unfortunately, more recently we've gone backwards again, at least a couple of steps backwards. First, under . . . well, I could blame every one of these presidents and politicians, and Reagan wasn't perfect by any means either, but most recently Bush really accelerated that retreat and now Obama's taking it to extraordinary lengths far beyond what any other president has ever done before.

But, you know, I'm an entrepreneur, and so I'm an optimist. I do think it's possible to reverse that trend. I don't think we're yet in an irreversible decline, but I do think we're going to have to make some serious changes fairly soon. We're going bankrupt, for one thing. Unless we're willing to take that seriously and deal with it without raising taxes and choking off the enterprise of America, unless we're willing to deal with that, then I see decline as inevitable. But I'm still hopeful right now!

Palmer: Do you think that capitalism creates conformity or does it create space for diversity? I'm thinking about people who like kosher food or halal food or religious or cultural or sexual minorities . . .

Mackey: You've almost answered the question just by being able to list those things. Capitalism is ultimately people cooperating together to create value for other people, as well as for themselves. That's what capitalism is. There's of course an element of self-interest in it, as well. The key is being able to create value through cooperation and doing so for both yourself and for others. And that creates diversity of productive effort, because human beings are very diverse in their wants and desires. Capitalism, cooperating in the market, aims to satisfy those wants and desires. So that creates tremendous space for individuality. If you live in an authoritarian society some special interest group, whether a religious hierarchy or university intellectuals or some group of fanatics who think that they know what's best for everyone, can force their values on everyone else. They get to dictate to others. In a capitalistic society you have far more space for individuality. There's space for billions of flowers to grow and flourish in a capitalistic society, simply because human flourishing is ultimately the goal or end of capitalism, its greatest creation.

Palmer: What's your vision of a just, enterprising, prosperous future?

Mackey: What I'd like to see happen is first that the defenders of capitalism start to understand that the strategy they've been using has really played into the hands of their opponents. They've conceded the moral high ground and they've allowed the enemies of capitalism to paint it as an exploitative, greedy, selfish system that creates inequality, exploits workers, defrauds consumers, and is wrecking the environment while eroding communities. The defenders don't know how to respond to that because they've already conceded major ground to the critics of capitalism. Instead, they need to shift away from their obsession with self-interest and begin to see the value that capitalism creates, not merely for investors—although, of course, it does that, but the value it creates for all of the people who trade with business: it creates value for customers; it creates value for workers; it creates value for suppliers; it creates value for the society as a whole; it creates value for governments. I mean, where would our government be without a strong business sector that creates jobs and income and wealth that they can then tax? Not that I'm always thrilled with that, mind you.

Capitalism is a source of value. It's the most amazing vehicle for social cooperation that has ever existed. And that's the story we need to tell. We need to change the narrative. From an ethical standpoint, we need to change the narrative of capitalism, to show that it's about creating shared value, not for the few, but for everyone. If people could see that the way I see it, people would love capitalism in the way I love it.

Palmer: Thank you for your time.

Mackey: It's my pleasure, Tom.

Liberty and Dignity Explain the Modern World

By Deirdre N. McCloskey

In this essay, the economic historian and social critic Deirdre McCloskey argues that the growth of modern capitalism and the world it made possible cannot be adequately explained by "material factors," as generations of historians have sought to do. It was a change in how people thought about business, exchange, innovation, and profit that created modern capitalism and liberated women, gay people, religious dissenters, and the previously downtrodden masses whose lives were brutal, painful, and short before the invention and commercialization of modern agriculture, medicine, electricity, and the other accessories of modern capitalist life.

Deirdre N. McCloskey is a professor of economics, history, English, and communication at the University of Illinois at Chicago. She is the author of thirteen books on economics, economic history, statistics, rhetoric, and literature, as well as a memoir, Crossing. *She was co-editor of the* Journal of Economic History *and has published extensively in academic journals. Her latest book, just out, is* Bourgeois Dignity: Why Economics Can't Explain the Modern World.

A change in how people *honored* markets and innovation caused the Industrial Revolution, and then the modern world. The old conventional wisdom, by contrast, has no place for attitudes about trade and innovation, and no place for liberal thought. The old materialist story says that the Industrial Revolution came from material causes, from investment or theft, from higher saving rates or from imperialism. You've heard it: "Europe is rich because of its empires"; "The United States was built on the backs of slaves"; "China is getting rich because of trade."

But what if the Industrial Revolution was sparked instead by changes in the way people *thought*, and especially by how they thought about each other? Suppose steam engines and computers came from a new *honor* for innovators—not from piling brick on brick, or dead African on dead African?

Economists and historians are starting to realize that it took much, much more than theft or capital accumulation to ignite the Industrial Revolution—it took a big shift in how Westerners thought about commerce and innovation. People had to start liking "creative destruction," the new idea that replaces the old. It's like music. A new band gets a new idea in rock music, and replaces the old if enough people freely adopt the new. If the old music is thought to be worse, it is "destroyed" by the creativity. In the same way, electric lights "destroyed" kerosene lamps, and computers "destroyed" typewriters. To our good.

The correct history goes like this: Until the Dutch around 1600 or the English around 1700 changed their thinking, you got honor in only two ways, by being a soldier or being a priest, in the castle or in the church. People who merely bought and sold things for a living, or innovated, were scorned as sinful cheaters. A jailer in the 1200s rejected a rich man's pleas for mercy: "Come, Master Arnaud Teisseire, you have wallowed in such opulence! *How* could you be without sin?"

In 1800 the average income per person per day all over the planet was, in present-day money, anything from $1 to $5. Call it an average of $3 a day. Imagine living in present-day Rio or Athens or Johannesburg on $3 a day. (Some people do even now.) That's three-fourths of a cappuccino at Starbucks. It was and is appalling.

Then something changed, in Holland and then in England. The revolutions and reformations of Europe, 1517 to 1789, gave voice to ordinary people outside the bishops and aristocrats. Europeans and then others came to *admire* entrepreneurs like Ben Franklin and Andrew Carnegie and Bill Gates. The middle class started to be viewed as *good*, and started to be allowed to do good, and to do well. People signed on to a Middle-Class Deal that has characterized now-wealthy places such as Britain or Sweden or Hong Kong ever since: "Let me innovate and make piles and piles of money in the short run out of innovation, and in the long run I'll make *you* rich."

And that's what happened. Starting in the 1700s with Franklin's lightning rod and Watt's steam engine, and going nuts in the 1800s, and nuttier still in the 2000s, the West, which for centuries had lagged behind China and Islam, became astoundingly innovative.

Give the middle class dignity and liberty for the first time in human history and here's what you get: the steam engine, the automatic textile loom, the assembly line, the symphony orchestra, the railway, the corporation, abolitionism, the steam printing press, cheap paper, wide literacy, cheap steel, cheap plate glass, the modern university, the modern newspaper, clean water, reinforced concrete, the women's movement, the electric light, the elevator, the automobile, petroleum, vacations in Yellowstone, plastics, half a million new English-language books a year, hybrid corn, penicillin, the airplane, clean urban air, civil rights, open-heart surgery, and the computer.

The result was that uniquely in history the ordinary people, and especially the very poor, were made much, much better off—remember the Middle-Class Deal. The poorest five percent of Americans are now about as well off in air-conditioning and automobiles as the richest five percent of Indians.

Now we're seeing the same shift play out in China and India, 40 percent of the world's population. The big economic story of our times is not the Great Recession of 2007-09—unpleasant though it was. The big story is that the Chinese in 1978 and then the Indians in 1991 adopted liberal ideas in their economies, and welcomed creative destruction. Now their goods and services per person are quadrupling in every generation.

By now, in the numerous places that have adopted middle-class liberty and dignity, the average person makes and consumes over $100 a day. Remember: two centuries ago it was $3 a day, in the same prices. And that doesn't take account of the great improvement in the quality of many things, from electric lights to antibiotics. Young people in Japan and Norway and Italy are even in conservatively measured terms around thirty times better off in material circumstances than their great-great-great-great-great grandparents. All the other leaps into the modern world—more democracy, the liberation of women, improved life expectancy, greater education, spiritual growth, artistic explosion—are firmly attached to the Great Fact of modern history, the increase by 2,900 percent in food and education and travel.

It is so big, so unprecedented, the Great Fact, that it's impossible to see it as coming out of routine causes such as trade or exploitation or investment or imperialism. That's what economists are good at explaining: routine. Yet all the routines had occurred on a big scale in China and the Ottoman Empire, in Rome and South Asia. Slavery was common in the Middle East, trade was large in India, investment in Chinese canals and Roman roads was immense. Yet no Great Fact happened. Something must be deeply wrong with explanations of the usual economic sort.

In other words, depending exclusively on economic materialism to explain the modern world, whether left-wing historical materialism or right-wing economics, is mistaken. Ideas of human dignity and liberty did the trick. As the economic historian Joel Mokyr puts it, "economic change in all periods depends, more than most economists think, on what people believe." The gigantic material changes were the outcome, not the cause. It was ideas, or "rhetoric," that caused our enrichment, and with it our modern liberties.

Competition and Cooperation

By David Boaz

In this essay, think tank executive and pundit David Boaz shows the relationship between competition and cooperation, which are often presented as stark alternatives: a society is organized according to one principle or the other. To the contrary, as Boaz explains, in capitalist economic orders people compete in order to cooperate with others.

David Boaz is the executive vice president of the Cato Institute and an advisor to Students For Liberty. He is the author of Libertarianism: A Primer *and editor of fifteen other books, including* The Libertarian Reader: Classic and Contemporary Writings from Lao Tzu to Milton Friedman. *He has written for newspapers such as the* New York Times, *the* Wall Street Journal, *and the* Washington Post, *is a frequent commentator on television and radio, and blogs regularly for* Cato@Liberty, The Guardian, The Australian, *and the* Encyclopedia Britannica.

Defenders of the market process often stress the benefits of competition. The competitive process allows for constant testing, experimenting, and adapting in response to changing situations. It keeps businesses constantly on their toes to serve consumers. Both analytically and empirically, we can see that competitive systems produce better results than centralized or monopoly systems. That's why, in books, newspaper articles, and television appearances, advocates of free markets stress the importance of the competitive marketplace and oppose restrictions on competition.

But too many people listen to the praise for *competition* and hear words like *hostile*, *cutthroat*, or *dog-eat-dog*. They wonder whether cooperation wouldn't be better than such an antagonistic posture toward the world. Billionaire investor George Soros, for instance, writes in the *Atlantic Monthly*, "Too much competition and too little cooperation can cause intolerable inequities and instability." He goes on to say that his "main point . . . is that cooperation is as much a part of the system as competition, and the slogan 'survival of the fittest' distorts this fact."

Now it should be noted that the phrase "survival of the fittest" is rarely used by advocates of freedom and free markets. It was coined to describe the process of biological evolution and to refer to the survival of the traits that were best suited to the environment; it may well be applicable to the competition of enterprises in the market, but it certainly is never intended to imply the survival of only the fittest individuals in a capitalist system. It is not the friends but the enemies of the market process who use the term "survival of the fittest" to describe economic competition.

What needs to be made clear is that those who say that human beings "are made for cooperation, not competition" fail to recognize that the market is cooperation. Indeed, as discussed below, it is people competing to cooperate.

Individualism and Community

Similarly, opponents of classical liberalism have been quick to accuse liberals of favoring "atomistic" individualism, in which each person is an island unto himself, out only for his own profit with no regard for the needs or wants of others. E. J. Dionne, Jr., of the *Washington Post* has written that modern libertarians believe that "individuals come into the world as fully formed adults who should be held responsible for their actions from the moment of their birth." Columnist Charles Krauthammer wrote in a review of Charles Murray's *What It Means to Be a Libertarian* that until Murray came along the libertarian vision was "a race of rugged individualists each living in a mountaintop cabin with a barbed wire fence and a 'No Trespassing' sign outside." How he neglected to include "each armed to the teeth" I can't imagine.

Of course, nobody actually believes in the sort of "atomistic individualism" that professors and pundits like to deride. We do live together and work in groups. How one could be an atomistic individual in our complex modern society is not clear: would that mean eating only what you grow, wearing what you make, living in a house you build for yourself, restricting yourself to natural medicines you extract from plants? Some critics of capitalism or advocates of "back to nature"—like the Unabomber, or Al Gore if he really meant what he wrote in *Earth in the Balance*—might endorse such a plan. But few libertarians would want to move to a desert island and renounce the benefits of what Adam Smith called the Great Society, the complex and productive society made possible by social interaction. One would think, therefore, that sensible journalists would stop, look at the words they typed, and think to themselves, "I must have misrepresented this position. I should go back and read the libertarian writers again."

In our time this canard—about isolation and atomism—has been very damaging to advocates of the market process. We ought to make it clear that we agree with George Soros that "cooperation is as much a part of the system as competition." In fact, we consider cooperation so essential to human flourishing that we don't just want to talk about it; we want to create social institutions that make it possible. That is what property rights, limited government, and the rule of law are all about.

In a free society individuals enjoy natural, imprescriptible rights and must live up to their general obligation to respect the rights of other individuals. Our other obligations are those we choose to assume by contract. It is not just coincidental that a society based on the rights of life, liberty, and property also produces social peace and material well-being. As John Locke, David Hume, and other classical-liberal philosophers demonstrate, we need a system of rights to produce social cooperation, without which people can achieve very little. Hume wrote in his *Treatise of Human Nature* that the circumstances confronting humans are (1) our self-interestedness, (2) our necessarily limited generosity toward others, and (3) the scarcity of resources available to fulfill our needs. Because of those circumstances, it is necessary for us to cooperate with others and to have rules of justice—especially regarding property and exchange—to define how we can do so. Those rules establish who has the right to decide how to use a particular piece of property. In the absence of well-defined property rights, we would face constant conflict over that issue. It is our agreement on property rights that allows us to undertake the complex social tasks of cooperation and coordination by which we achieve our purposes.

It would be nice if love could accomplish that task, without all the emphasis on self-interest and individual rights, and many opponents of liberalism have offered an appealing vision of society based on universal benevolence. But as Adam Smith pointed out, "in civilized society [man] stands at all times in need of the cooperation and assistance of great multitudes," yet in his whole life he could never befriend a small fraction of the number of people whose cooperation he needs. If we depended entirely on benevolence to produce cooperation, we simply couldn't undertake complex tasks. Reliance on other people's self-interest, in a system of well-defined property rights and free exchange, is the only way to organize a society more complicated than a small village.

Civil Society

We want to associate with others to achieve instrumental ends—producing more food, exchanging goods, developing new technology—but also because we feel a deep human need for connectedness, for love and friendship and community. The associations we form with others make up what we call civil society. Those associations can take an amazing variety of forms—families, churches, schools, clubs, fraternal societies, condominium associations, neighborhood groups, and the myriad forms of commercial society, such as partnerships, corporations, labor unions, and trade associations. All of these associations serve human needs in different ways. Civil society may be broadly defined as all the natural and voluntary associations in society.

Some analysts distinguish between commercial and nonprofit organizations, arguing that businesses are part of the market, not of civil society; but I follow the tradition that the real distinction is between associations that are coercive—the state—and those that are natural or voluntary—everything else. Whether a particular association is established to make a profit or to achieve some other purpose, the key characteristic is that our participation in it is voluntarily chosen.

With all the contemporary confusion about civil society and "national purpose," we should remember F. A. Hayek's point that the associations within civil society are created to achieve a particular purpose, but civil society as a whole has no single purpose; it is the undesigned, spontaneously emerging result of all those purposive associations.

The Market as Cooperation

The market is an essential element of civil society. The market arises from two facts: that human beings can accomplish more in cooperation with others than individually and that we can recognize this. If we were a species for whom cooperation was not more productive than isolated work, or if we were unable to discern the benefits of cooperation, then we would remain isolated and atomistic. But worse than that, as Ludwig von Mises explained, "Each man would have been forced to view all other men as his enemies; his craving for the satisfaction of his own appetites would have brought him into an implacable conflict with all his neighbors." Without the possibility of mutual benefit from cooperation and the division of labor, neither feelings of sympathy and friendship nor the market order itself could arise.

Throughout the market system individuals and firms compete to cooperate better. General Motors and Toyota compete to cooperate with me in achieving my goal of transportation. AT&T and MCI compete to cooperate with me in achieving my goal of communication with others. Indeed, they compete so aggressively for my business that I have cooperated with yet another communications firm that provides me with peace of mind via an answering machine.

Critics of markets often complain that capitalism encourages and rewards self-interest. In fact, people are self-interested under any political system. Markets channel their self-interest in socially beneficent directions. In a free market, people achieve their own purposes by finding out what others want and trying to offer it. That may mean several people working together to build a fishing net or a road. In a more complex economy, it means seeking one's own profit by offering goods or services that satisfy the needs or desires of others. Workers and entrepreneurs who best satisfy those needs will be rewarded; those who don't will soon find out and be encouraged to copy their more successful competitors or try a new approach.

All the different economic organizations we see in a market are experiments to find better ways of cooperating to achieve mutual purposes. A system of property rights, the rule of law, and minimal government allow maximum scope for people to experiment with new forms of cooperation. The development of the corporation allowed larger economic tasks to be undertaken than individuals or partnerships could achieve. Organizations such as condominium associations, mutual funds, insurance companies, banks, worker-owned cooperatives, and more are attempts to solve particular economic problems by new forms of association. Some of these forms are discovered to be inefficient; many of the corporate conglomerates in the 1960s, for instance, proved to be unmanageable, and shareholders lost money. The rapid feedback of the market process provides incentives for successful forms of organization to be copied and unsuccessful forms to be discouraged.

Cooperation *is* as much a part of capitalism as competition. Both are essential elements of the simple system of natural liberty, and most of us spend far more of our time cooperating with partners, coworkers, suppliers, and customers than we do competing.

Life would indeed be nasty, brutish, and short if it were solitary. Fortunately for all of us, in capitalist society it isn't.

For-Profit Medicine and the Compassion Motive

By Tom G. Palmer

In this essay the editor of this volume offers a personal meditation based on his experience of treatment for pain. It is not offered as a general doctrine, nor is it a contribution to social science. It's an attempt to clarify the relationship between business enterprise and compassion.

For-profit medicine must be a terrible and immoral thing. After all, I hear it attacked as such all the time. Indeed, as I write this I'm listening to a bitter attack on private hospitals over the Canadian Broadcasting Corporation. When doctors, nurses, and hospital administrators care only about their income, compassion is replaced by cold-hearted selfishness, many people say. But I just got a new view of the issue when I found myself having to visit two hospitals—one for-profit, the other nonprofit—for relief from a painful and crippling condition.

I recently suffered from a ruptured disk in my spine that caused kinds of pain that I had never imagined possible. I visited a specialist at a local for-profit hospital, and he arranged for me to get an MRI (magnetic resonance imaging) scan within an hour at a nearby for-profit radiology clinic. Then he arranged for me to have an epidural injection to reduce the inflammation of the nerves coming into the spinal column, which were the source of the pains. I was in such agony that I could barely move at all. The for-profit pain clinic at the for-profit hospital I visited was staffed by doctors and nurses who showed me extraordinary kindness and treated me with gentleness. After the nurse had made sure that I understood the procedure and that I could understand all the directions, the doctor who administered the epidural injection introduced herself, explained every step, and then proceeded with both notable professionalism and evident concern for my well-being.

Fast forward a few weeks. My condition, although still painful and debilitating, was greatly improved. My doctor recommended another epidural injection to advance me even more toward a normal state. Unfortunately, the for-profit pain clinic was booked up completely for three weeks. I didn't want to wait that long and called some other hospitals in the area. A very well-known and highly regarded nonprofit hospital could fit me in in two days. I gladly made an appointment.

When I got to the nonprofit hospital, I spoke first with some helpful retired ladies and gentlemen who were wearing neat volunteer uniforms. They were clearly benevolent people, as one might expect in a nonprofit hospital. Then I hobbled with my cane to the pain clinic, where I signed in with the desk. A nurse came out and announced my name and after I identified myself, sat down next to me in the lobby. The interview took place while I was surrounded with strangers. Thankfully, there were no embarrassing questions. I noticed that the other nurses were actually ordering patients about in the imperative voice. One nurse told a lady who was clearly in pain to sit in another chair and after the patient said she was more comfortable where she was, the nurse pointed to the other chair and said, "No. Sit!" When that same nurse approached me, I think that my look told her that I had no intention of being treated like an enrollee in obedience school. Wordlessly, she pointed at the examination room, which I entered.

The administering doctor walked in. No introduction. No name. No hand to shake. He looked at my file, muttered to himself, and told me to sit on the bed, pull down my pants, and hoist my shirt. I told him that the procedure had been done before while I was lying on my side, and that that position was more comfortable, since sitting was quite painful. He said that he preferred it with me sitting. I responded that I preferred to lie on my side. He said that sitting allowed better access, which was at least a reason that appealed to my interests as well as his, so I acquiesced. Then, unlike the doctor in the for-profit hospital, he slammed in the needle and injected the medication with such surprising and agonizing force that it caused me to let loose a real yell, quite unlike my previous experience. Then he removed the needle, made a note in his file, and disappeared. The nurse handed me a sheet of paper and pointed the way out. I paid and left.

Profit and Compassion

That's too small a set of experiences on the basis of which to compare for-profit and nonprofit medicine. But it may suggest something about the profit motive and its relation to compassion. It's not that for-profit hospitals alone attract the kindly and compassionate, since the elderly volunteers in the nonprofit hospital were surely kindly and compassionate. But I can't help thinking that the doctors and nurses who worked in a for-profit pain clinic in a for-profit hospital had some incentive to exercise their compassion at work. After all, if I need additional treatment or if I find myself asked for a recommendation, I'm going to think of the for-profit hospital. But I will neither go back to, nor recommend, the nonprofit hospital, and I think I know why: the doctors and nurses there had no reason to want me to. And now I also understand why the nonprofit hospital could fit me in so quickly. I doubt they had many repeat customers.

The experience does not suggest that profits are a necessary or even sufficient condition for compassion, benevolence, or courtesy. I work at a nonprofit organization, which is dependent on the continued support of a wide base of donors. If I were to fail to fulfill my fiduciary obligations to them, they would stop supporting my work. It so happens that I and my colleagues work there because we share the same concerns as the donors, so the arrangement works out harmoniously. But when the donors, the employees, and the "clients" (whether people in pain or journalists and educators in need of information and insight) don't all share the same values or goals, as in the nonprofit hospital, the profit motive acts powerfully to bring those goals into harmony.

Profits earned in the context of well-defined and enforced legal rights (as distinguished from the profits that accrue to being a brilliant thief) may provide the foundation not of coldness, but of compassion. The search for profit requires that the doctor consider the interests of the patient by putting himself or herself into the patient's position, to imagine the suffering of others, to have compassion. In a free-market economy, the profit motive may be but another name for the compassion motive.

Section II

Voluntary Interaction and Self-Interest

The Paradox of Morality

By Mao Yushi
(*Translated by Jude Blanchette*)

In this essay, the Chinese economist and intellectual and so-cial entrepreneur Mao Yushi (茅于轼) explains the role that markets play in bringing about concord and cooperation. He reveals the benefits of the search for low prices and profits by those engaging in exchange by contrasting such "self-interested" behavior with the fantasies advanced by critics of capitalism. He draws his examples from both China's literary heritage and from his experiences (and those of millions of other Chinese people) during China's disastrous experiment in abolishing capitalism.

Mao Yushi is founder and chairman of the Unirule Institute, based in Beijing, China. He is the author of several books and many scholarly and popular articles, has taught economics at a number of universities, established some of the very first non-state charities and independent self-help organizations in China, and is well known as a courageous champion of liberty. In the 1950s he was punished through forced labor, exile, "re-education," and near starvation for saying, "If we have nowhere to buy pork, then pork prices should rise," and "If Chairman Mao wants to meet a scientist, who should visit whom?" And in 2011, just before this book went to press, at the age of 82, he wrote a public essay that was published in Caixin online called "Returning Mao Zedong to Human Form" (把毛泽东还原成人). That essay earned him numerous death threats and a greater reputation as a voice of honesty and justice. Mao Yushi is one of the great libertarian figures in the contemporary world and has worked tirelessly to bring libertarian ideas and the experience of freedom to the people of China and the wider world.

Conflict of Interest in The Land of Gentlemen

Between the eighteenth and nineteenth centuries, Chinese author Li Ruzhen wrote a novel titled *Flowers in the Mirror*. The book describes a person named Tang Ao who, owing to a career setback, follows his brother-in-law overseas. During the voyage, he visits many different countries that contain fantastic and exotic sights and sounds. The first country they visit is "The Land of Gentlemen."

All of the inhabitants of The Land of Gentlemen intentionally suffer so that they may ensure the benefit of others. The eleventh chapter of the novel describes a bailiff (Li Ruzhen here intentionally uses the Chinese character as it was understood in Ancient China, where bailiffs had special privileges and often bullied the common people) who encountered the following situation while buying goods:

> The bailiff, after examining a handful of goods, says to the seller, "Friend, you have such high quality goods, yet your price is so low. How can I be at ease while taking advantage of you? If you don't raise the price, then you will stop us from doing any further trade."
>
> The seller responded: "Coming to my shop is a favor to me. It has been a saying that the seller asks a price up to the sky, and the buyer responds to it by going down to earth. My price is up to the sky, but you still want me to raise it. It's hard for me to agree. It's better to visit another store to buy goods."
>
> The bailiff, after hearing the response of the seller, responded: "You have given a low price to such high-quality goods. Won't this mean a loss for you? We should act without deception and with equanimity. Can it not be said that all of us have an abacus built into us?" After quarrelling for some time, the seller continued to insist that the price not be raised, while the bailiff, in a fit of anger, purchased only half of the goods he had originally intended to purchase. Just as he was about to take his leave, the seller blocked his way. At this point, along came two old men who,

after assessing the situation, settled the transaction by ordering the bailiff to take 80 percent of the goods and leave.

The book next describes another transaction in which the buyer thinks the asking price for the goods is too low as the quality is high, while the seller insists that the goods lack freshness and should be considered ordinary. In the end, the buyer chooses from the worst of the seller's goods, causing the crowd nearby to accuse him of unfairness, so the buyer takes half from the high-quality pile and half from the low-quality pile. In a third transaction, both parties begin to quarrel while assessing the weight and quality of silver. The party paying with silver sternly says that his silver is of poor quality and inadequate weight, while the party being paid states that the silver is of superior quality and weight. As the payer has already taken leave, the party being paid finds himself obligated to give what silver he thinks is extra to a beggar visiting from a foreign land.

There are two points raised in the novel that are worth exploring further.

The first is that when both parties decide to give up their share of the profits or insist that their share of the profits is too high, an argument ensues. In the arguments we encounter in real life, most stem from us pursuing our own interests. As a result, we often make the mistake of assuming that if we were to always side with the other party, such disputes wouldn't occur. But in The Land of Gentlemen, we can see that taking the interests of others as the basis of our decisions also leads to conflict, and as a result, we still must search for the logical foundation of a harmonious and coordinated society.

Going a step further in our investigation, we recognize that in business deals in the real world both parties to a transaction seek their own gain, and through negotiations over terms (including price and quality) both sides can reach agreement. By contrast, in The Land of Gentlemen, such agreement is impossible. In the novel, the author must enlist an old man and a beggar and even resorts to compulsion to resolve the conflict.[30] Here we encounter a profound and important truth: negotiations in which both parties are seeking their personal gain can reach equilibrium, whereas if both parties are looking towards the interests of the other party, they will never reach a consensus. What's more, this would create a society always at odds with itself. This fact goes strongly against the expectations of most. Because The Land of Gentleman is unable to realize a balance in the relations between its inhabitants, it eventually turns into the Land of the Inconsiderate and Coarse. Because The Land of Gentlemen is geared towards looking after the interest of others, it is a breeding ground for vile characters. When the Gentlemen fail to conclude an exchange, the Inconsiderate and Coarse are able to gain advantage by leveraging the fact that Gentlemen seek profit by subverting their own interests. If things were to continue in that way, the Gentlemen would likely die out and be replaced by the Inconsiderate and Coarse.

From the above point we can see that humans can only co-operate when they seek their own interests. That is the secure foundation on which humanity is able to strive for an ideal world. If humankind were to directly and exclusively seek the benefit of others, no ideals could be realized.

Of course, using reality as our starting point, in order to re-duce conflict, we must all pay attention to our fellow man and find ways to restrain our own selfish desires. But if attention to the interests of others were to become the goal of *all* behavior, it would generate the same conflict as Li Ruzhen described in The Land of Gentlemen. There are perhaps those who say the more comical elements of life in The Land of Gentlemen could not occur in the real world, but as the book gradually makes evident, events in the real world and those in The Land of Gentlemen have similar causes. To put it another way, both the real world and The Land of Gentlemen lack clarity regarding the principle of the pursuit of self-interest.

What are the motives of the inhabitants of the Land of Gentlemen? We must first ask, "Why do humans want to ex-change?" Whether it is primitive barter exchange or modern society's exchange of goods for currency, the motive behind exchange is to improve one's situation, to make one's life more convenient and more comfortable. Without that motivation, why would individuals choose exchange over toiling on their own? All of the material enjoyments we receive, from needles and thread to refrigerators and color TVs, are only available through exchange. If people did not exchange, each individual would only be able to plant grains and cotton in the countryside, to use mud bricks to build houses, and struggle to wrest from the soil all the goods one needs to exist. In such a way one might be able to eke out a living as our ancestors did for tens of thousands of years. But we would certainly not enjoy any of the benefits offered by today's modern civilization.

The people in The Land of Gentlemen already have a state and a market, which shows that they've already abandoned economic self-sufficiency and have instead chosen to follow the road of exchange in order to improve their material circumstances. That being the case, why is it that they refuse to think of their own interests when engaging in economic exchanges? Of course, if from the start the point of exchange is to lessen one's own advantage and promote the advantage of others, "gentlemanly" behavior might, perhaps, occur. However, as anyone knows who participates in an exchange, or who has experience with exchange, both parties to an exchange participate for their own benefit, while those who act contrary to their own self-interest during the course of an exchange suffer from an incoherence of motives.

Is It Feasible to Establish a Society Based On Mutual Benefit Without Price Negotiations?

During the period in which the life and deeds of Lei Feng[31] were being promoted in China, one could often see on television the image of one of Lei Feng's committed and kind emulators repairing pots and pans for an assembly of people. One would then notice a long line forming in front of him, with each person holding worn-out utensils in need of repair. The intended message of these images was to encourage others to emulate that kind-hearted follower of Lei Feng, and to focus the public on his example. Notice that if it weren't for the long line of people, the propaganda would have no power to persuade. We should also take note that those who queued to have their pots and pans repaired were not there to learn from Lei Feng; to the contrary, they were there to seek their own gain at the expense of others.

While such propaganda may teach some to do good deeds for others, at the same time it is teaching even more how to benefit personally from the work of others. In the past, it was thought that propaganda calling on the people to work in the service of others without repayment could improve social morals. Yet that is most certainly a great misunderstanding, for those who will learn how to seek some type of personal advantage will greatly outnumber those who learn how to work in the service of others.

From the perspective of economic gains, a universal obligation to serve others is wasteful. Those attracted to the offer of free repair services are quite likely carrying damaged items that are not really worth repairing, perhaps even items taken directly from the trash. But because the price of fixing those items is now zero, the scarce time devoted to repairing them will increase, as will the scarce materials used for their repair. As the burden to fix these items rests on the shoulders of others, the only cost to the average person seeking a free repair is the time it takes to queue. From the vantage point of society as a whole, all of the time, effort, and materials used to repair those damaged items will yield some barely usable pots and pans. If the time and materials were instead used on more productive activities, it would certainly create more value for society. From the perspective of economic efficiency and overall wellbeing, such obligatory and uncompensated repair work almost certainly does more harm than good.

What's more, if yet another kind-hearted student of Lei Feng were to offer to take the place in the queue of one of the people holding pots waiting for free repair services, thus freeing that poor person from the tedium of queuing, the line for those waiting to have his or her items fixed would become even longer. That would indeed be an absurd sight, with one group standing in line so that an additional group doesn't have to. Such a system of obligation presupposes a group willing to be served as a precondition. Such an ethic of service cannot be universal. Obviously those who boast about the superiority of such a system of mutual service without prices have not thought this through.

The obligation to repair the goods of others has an additional unanticipated result. If those who were formerly engaged in the repair trade are crowded out by the students of Lei Feng, they will lose their jobs and suffer hardship.

In no way do I oppose the study of Lei Feng, as he helped those in need, which for society is a positive, even a necessary, activity. However, the requirement that the service of others be obligatory creates incoherence and disorder and distorts the voluntary spirit of Lei Feng.

In our society there are those who are quite cynical, and who detest a society that, in their estimation, elevates money above all else. They think that those with money are insufferable and that the rich view themselves above the rest of society, while the poor suffer for the sake of humanity. They believe that money warps the normal relations between mankind. As a result, they desire to create a society based on mutual service, free from talk of money and prices. That would be a society where peasants plant food without thought of reward; where workers weave cloth for all, also without reward; where barbers cut hair for free; etc. Is such an ideal society practical?

For an answer, we need to turn to the economic theory of resource allocation, which requires a digression of some length. To make it easier, we could start with a thought experiment. Consider a barber. Currently, men get their hair cut every three to four weeks, but if haircuts were free, they might go to the barber every week. Charging money for hair cuts better utilizes the labor of the barber. In the market, the price of the barber's services determines the share of society's labor devoted to that profession. If the state keeps the price of a haircut low, then the number of those seeking haircuts will increase, and accordingly the number of barbers will also need to increase and other jobs must be reduced if the total labor force is held constant. What's true of barbers is true of other professions.

In many of China's rural areas, the offering of free services is quite common. If someone wants to build a new house, their relatives and friends all come to help with the construction. That usually happens without payment, save for a large meal served to all those who helped. The next time one of the beneficiary's friends builds a new house, the one who benefited the first time offers free labor as a form of repayment. Repairmen often fix electrical appliances without charging, expecting only a gift during the Chinese New Year holiday as compensation. Such non-monetary exchanges cannot accurately measure the value of the services offered. Consequently, the value of labor is not efficiently developed, and the division of labor in society is not encouraged. Money and prices play an important role in the development of society. No one should hope to replace emotions such as love and friendship with money. It does not follow, though, that love and friendship can replace money. We cannot do away with money just because we fear that it will erode the bonds of human emotion. In fact, prices expressed in money are the only method available for determining how to allocate resources to their most highly valued uses. If we maintain both monetary prices and our highest emotions and values, we can still hope to build a society that is both efficient and humane.

The Balance of Self-Interests

Suppose that A and B need to divide two apples before they can eat them. A makes the first move and grabs the bigger of the two. B bitterly asks A, "How could you be so selfish?" to which A retorts, "If it were you to have grabbed first, which one would you have chosen?" B responds, "I would have grabbed the smaller apple." Laughing, A responds, "If that is the case, then the way I selected is perfectly in line with your wishes."

In that scenario, A took advantage of B, as B was following the principle of "placing the interest of others above oneself," while A was not. If only one segment of society follows that principle while others do not, the former is assured to suffer losses, while the latter will profit. If that continues unchecked, it is bound to lead to conflict. Clearly, if only some of the people put the interests of others before themselves, then in the end this system will merely generate conflict and disorder.

If *both* A and B look to the interest of the other party, then the above mentioned apple problem would be impossible to resolve. As both would look to eat the smaller one, a new problem would arise, just as we saw in The Land of Gentlemen. What is true of A and B would be true of everyone. If all of society, save for one person, followed the principle of explicitly benefiting others, the entire society would serve at this person's pleasure; such a system would be possible, logically speaking. But if that person were in turn to become a practitioner of the above-mentioned principle of serving others, then the society would cease to exist as a society, that is, as a system of cooperation. The principle of serving others is generally feasible only under the condition that looking after the interests of the whole society could be delegated to others. But from the perspective of the entire globe, that would be impossible unless the responsibility for looking after the interests of the planet's population could be delegated to the moon.

The reason for that incoherence is because from the vantage point of society as a whole, there is no difference between "others" and "oneself." Of course, to a specific John or Jane Doe, "oneself" is "oneself," while "others" are "others," and the former shouldn't be confused with the latter. However, from a societal perspective, every person is at the same time "oneself" and an "other." When the principle of "serve others before serving oneself" is applied to Person A, Person A must first contemplate the gains and losses of others. Yet when the same principle is adopted by Person B, *Person A becomes the person whose interest is placed as primary.* To members of the same society, the question of whether they should think of others first, or others should think of them first leads directly to confusion and contradiction. Therefore, the principle of selflessness in this context is logically incoherent and contradictory, and therefore could not serve the function of solving the many problems that arise in human relationships. That, of course, is not to say that the spirit animating them is never worthy of being commended, or that such other-regarding behavior is not commendable, but rather that it could not provide the universal basis by which members of society look to secure their mutual interest.

Those who lived through the Cultural Revolution will remember that when the slogan "Struggle Against Selfishness, Criticize Revisionism" (dousi pixiu) echoed through the country, the numbers of conspirators and careerists were at their peak. At that time, most of China's common people (laobaixing) could actually believe that "Struggle Against Selfishness, Criticize Revisionism" could become a societal norm, and as a result they did their utmost to follow its strictures. At the same time, opportunists used the slogan as a means to take advantage of others. They used the campaign against exploitation as an excuse to raid the homes of others and place the property of others in their own pockets. They called on others to strike down selfishness, and for the sake of the revolution to admit that they were traitors, spies, or counter-revolutionaries and thus have a stroke added to their record of demerits. Without a thought, such opportunists would place others in a position where the lives of those others were at stake, all in an effort to secure for themselves an official government position. Thus far, we've analyzed the theoretical problems with the principle of "serve others before oneself," but the history of the Cultural Revolution further proves the contradiction of that principle when it is put into practice.

The Cultural Revolution has faded into memory, but we should remember that at that time all slogans were subjected to criticism and scrutiny. That is no longer the case, for the question of what principle is best when dealing with problems in society has, it seems, been exempted from scrutiny. We still often use the old propaganda to call on the people to resolve disputes, and even when cases are heard in court, those out-of-date methods still hold considerable influence.

Those readers who are adept at thought experiments will no doubt have additional questions to ask about the above-mentioned problem of how best to allocate the apples between the two individuals. If we agree that "serve others before oneself" cannot as a rule solve the problem of how best to distribute two apples, does it follow that there is no better way to do so? Recall that there is one small apple and one large apple, and there are only two individuals participating in the allocation. Could it be that even the legendary Chinese immortals would find themselves unable to devise a suitable solution?

In an exchange society, the above-mentioned conundrum is indeed soluble. The two individuals can first consult with one another in order to resolve the dilemma. For example, suppose that A selects the bigger apple, with the understanding that B is entitled to take home the bigger apple when they next meet; or if in return for A taking the bigger apple, B receives some form of compensation. A payment would help to resolve the difficulty. In an economy utilizing money, there would certainly be parties willing to use the latter method. Starting with an offer of a small amount in compensation (say, one cent), the amount could gradually be increased until the other party was willing to accept the smaller apple, plus compensation. If the initial sum is quite small, we can assume that both parties would prefer to take the larger apple and to pay a small amount of compensation. As the compensation increases it would reach a point where one of the two parties would accept the smaller apple plus the compensation. We can say with certainty that if both parties rationally evaluate the problem, they will find a method to solve the dispute. And this is a way to resolve peacefully the conflicting interests of both parties.

Thirty years after China's Reform and Opening, the question of wealth and poverty has been raised yet again, with animosity towards the rich growing with each day. During the period when class struggle was emphasized, at the start of each mass movement, the suffering of the past was contrasted to the happiness of the present. The previous society was denounced, and previous exploitation was used as a seed to mobilize the hatred of the people. When the Cultural Revolution began in 1966 (a movement to sweep away the evils of the old class system), in many areas the descendants of the landowning class were buried alive, even though most of the landowners themselves were already dead. No one was spared: neither the old nor the young, nor even the women and children. People said, just as there is no love without cause, so there is no hatred without reason. Where did this spirit of enmity towards the children of the landowning class come from? It came from the fervent belief that those descendants of the landed class had relied upon exploitation to create their place in the world. Today, the gap between the rich and the poor has become more evident. And while there are admittedly those who have used illegal methods to gain wealth, in any society a gap between the rich and the poor is an unavoidable phenomenon. Even in developed countries where illegal channels are strictly limited, a gap between the rich and the poor commonly exists.

The logic behind the resentment of the rich is flawed. If one were resentful of the rich because one had not yet become rich, then the best strategy one could adopt would be first to overthrow the rich, and then wait until such a time that one had oneself become wealthy, after which one would advocate the protection of the rights of the wealthy. For a certain group of individuals, this indeed would be the most rational way forward. But for society as a whole, there is no way to coordinate this process so that all of the members of society could become wealthy at the same pace. Some will become wealthy before others; if we wait for all to become wealthy at the same rate, none will ever achieve wealth. The opposition to the rich is without justification, for the poor will only have a chance to become rich if the rights that allow anyone—and everyone—to gain wealth are guaranteed; if the fruits of one's labor are not infringed upon; and if the right of property is respected. A society in which more and more individuals attain wealth and agree that "to get rich is glorious" is, in fact, something that *can* be built.

The Chinese scholar Li Ming once wrote that dividing people into two groups, "rich" and "poor," is the wrong way to distinguish between the two. Rather, it should be those *with* rights and those *without* rights. What he meant was that in modern society, the question of rich and poor is really a question of rights. The rich have gotten that way because they have rights, while the poor don't. What he meant by rights must be human rights, not privileges. It cannot be the case that all citizens can have access to privilege. Only a small minority can have access to privileges. If we want to resolve the question of the rich and the poor, we should first establish equal human rights for all. Li Ming's analysis is profound and thorough.

The Moral Logic of Equality and Inequality in Market Society

By Leonid V. Nikonov

In this essay, Russian philosopher Leonid Nikonov subjects the idea of "equality" in exchange to critical scrutiny and finds that most anti-capitalistic criticisms that rest on claims about equality, whether of initial endowment, values, or outcomes, are incoherent.

Leonid Nikonov is a Lecturer in Philosophy at Altai State University in Barnaul, in the Russian Federation, where he teaches courses on social philosophy, ontology, theory of knowledge, and the philosophy of religion. He is currently working on a book on "Moral Measurements of Liberalism" and has published in a number of Russian academic publications. In 2010 he established and became director of the Center for the Philosophy of Freedom, which organizes conferences, debate tournaments, and other programs in Russia and Kazakhstan. He became further involved in such work after he won first place in the 2007 essay contest (in Russian) on "Global Capitalism and Human Freedom," a competition like that being sponsored in 2011 by Students For Liberty, and attended the summer school on freedom in Alushta, Ukraine. (The program was then organized as Cato.ru, and is now InLiberty.ru.) In 2011 he was invited to join the Mont Pelerin Society, which was founded in 1947 by 39 scholars to revive classical liberal thought, as their youngest member.

Markets don't necessarily generate equal outcomes, nor do they require equal endowments. That's not just a regrettable cost of having a market, though. Inequality is not merely a normal outcome of market exchange. It's a precondition of exchange, without which exchange would lack sense. To expect market exchanges, and thus societies in which wealth is allocated through the market, to result in equality is absurd. Equal basic rights, including equal freedom to exchange, are necessary for free markets, but free markets should not be expected to generate equal outcomes, nor do they rely on equality of conditions other than legal rights.

The ideal of equal exchange can refer to equality of initial endowments or to equality of outcomes. If the former sense is meant, only parties that are equal in every relevant sense could engage in equal exchange; any differential would unequalize the exchange, which is why some reject as inherently unequal (and thus unfair) labor contracts between employers and employees. In the latter sense, it could mean that equal values are exchanged, or that the outcomes of the exchange are equal in value. For example, if the same amount of goods of the same quality were to move from one party to the other, the exchange would satisfy the conditions of equality. Imagine a surrealistic scene in which two humanoids, totally like each other (i.e., devoid of personal differences relevantly constitutive of inequality), pass quite identical things between themselves. Setting aside any aesthetic revulsion we might feel at such an unnatural picture, common sense by itself should suggest that the very idea of equal *exchange* rests on a profound contradiction. Such an exchange changes nothing; it would not improve the position of either party, meaning neither party would have any reason to make it. (Karl Marx insisted that exchanges in the market were based on exchanges of equal values, which generated a nonsensical and incoherent economic theory.) Grounding market exchange on the principle of equality deprives exchange of its fundamental reason, which is to make the parties to exchange better off. The economics of exchange rests on a recognition of the unequal valuation of goods or services by the exchanging parties.

Considered ethically, however, the idea of equality may nonetheless be appealing for some. A common trait of many moral judgments is that they are formulated in purely deontic modality, that is, in the logic of duties alone. They are concerned only with what should be done, regardless of the logic of economics, or of what merely exists, or even of what will exist because of what (it may be asserted) must be done. According to Immanuel Kant, for example, a duty demands its realization, regardless of the results, consequences and even possibilities to do what must be done. To say that you must is to say that you can. Therefore even if such equality in exchange is economically absurd, it may still be (and is) upheld as a moral ideal.

Equality as a moral issue is a quite complicated matter. We can distinguish between those perspectives for which the achievement of equality is the dominant concern and those for which it is not; accordingly, the former are known as egalitarian perspectives and the latter as nonegalitarian perspectives. Nonegalitarians neither necessarily assert the undesirability of equality, nor need they assert the desirability of inequality; they merely reject the exclusive egalitarian focus on equality as a goal, to the exclusion of other goals, and especially the focus on assuring equality of material wealth. Classical liberal (or libertarian) nonegalitarians do assert the importance of a certain kind of equality, namely, equality of basic rights, which they hold to be inconsistent with equality of outcomes, so they could be considered egalitarians of a different sort. (Equality of rights is at the foundation of much of the experience of law, property, and toleration that people in modern and free societies take for granted.) Nonegalitarian libertarians and classical liberals defend their view as the purest or most consistent or most sustainable form of equality, but advocates of equality of wealth "distribution" generally claim that such libertarian equality is merely formal, equality in words, but not in deeds. (In that they have a point, in that legal equality is very much about what people think and how they act, rather than about describable states of the world or static distributions of assets. Whether such an approach to equality is merely formal, rather than substantive, depends on how one views the importance of legal procedures and standards of behavior.)

It's hardly unusual for difficult philosophical questions to be actively discussed before they are clearly formulated or properly posed. Philosophers of the East and the West propounded ethical doctrines for thousands of years before there was much systematic analysis of judgments regarding duty and performative logic. Such work was begun in earnest by David Hume and followed by Immanuel Kant and later by positivist philosophers such as George Moore, Alfred Ayer, Richard Hare and others; the investigation of performative and deontic logic is ongoing. Although the dispute between egalitarian and nonegalitarian stances is not limited merely to consideration of the proper logical relationship between equality and morality, understanding the relationship between equality and morality would be a worthy contribution to the ongoing and intense debate about whether forced redistribution of unequal wealth generated by market exchange is morally required or morally forbidden. (That is quite a separate issue from whether resources stolen from rightful owners, whether by rulers of states or by "free lance" criminals, should be returned to those who were despoiled.)

Let's consider the problem of the morality of equality through a simple question: why is equality, either of initial endowments or of outcomes, morally superior to inequality (or vice versa)? An honest attempt to arrive at an ethical resolution of the dispute requires that such a direct question should be addressed to both egalitarians and nonegalitarians.

The range of possible answers is limited. One might first try to establish that certain numerical proportions (of equality or inequality) are better than any others. For example, the ratio of X to Y is morally superior if the values of the variables are equal and morally inferior if not, i.e., if the ratio of "1:1" is superior to that of "1:2" (and, *a fortiori*, superior to "1:10"). In spite of what might seem like the evident clarity of such a position, however, the question of moral features is not so easily resolved. Values are not derived from statements of mathematical proportion, which are by themselves ethically neutral. It's quite arbitrary to assert the superiority of one mathematical ratio over another, rather like the curious practice of the Pythagoreans, who classified numbers as male, female, amicable, perfect, deficient, and so on.

Rather than directing attention to equality of either initial endowments or the outcomes of exchanges, it might make more sense to focus attention on the equality or inequality of one's personal moral status as the basis for evaluation of the relations (including exchanges) among persons. Thus: no person has a morally superior (or inferior) status to any other person or, alternatively, some people are morally superior (or inferior) to others. On such a foundation one might deduce the desirability or undesirability of insisting on equal initial endowments or outcomes. Both perspectives might converge on forced redistribution, either to eliminate or to establish inequality, and in both cases the central argument would be the moral status of the parties, regardless of the unbridgeable conceptual abyss between the very idea of moral status and the actual situations with which people deal.

So formulated, the central question would be about the relationship between human moral status, on the one hand, and the amount, quality, or value of goods to which a person has access, on the other. So we might follow up by asking why two equally morally significant persons must drink only the same amount, quality, or value of coffee in the morning? Or whether the charitable man and his stingy neighbor, both of equal moral standing (or are they?), should or should not own equally flourishing orchards producing equally valuable crops? Equal moral status seems not to have any obvious significance for equality of endowments, or of consumption, or of holdings. Consider the relationship of two chess players, both of whom are equally morally significant. Does their equal moral significance require that they must have the same skills, or that every game must end in a draw? Or does it require that they play by the same rules, which fact would entail no normative prescription that their games would have to end in draws. There is no direct connection between equal moral status and either initial endowments or particular outcomes.

If we focus on behavior and rules, rather than on endowments or outcomes, we find that states of affairs are judged by human behavior, by choices, and (in cases of criminality, especially) by intentions. How much money is in one person's pocket and whether that amount is greater or less than the sum in his or her neighbor's pocket is not itself a morally significant element in human life. What matters is how it got there. Both a tycoon and a taxi driver can be judged as just or unjust, depending on the compatibility of their actions with universal moral standards, such as whether they respect the rules of justice and the moral agency inherent in both themselves and in others. Praise and blame are not merited by wealth or poverty per se, but by the actions people take. Different positions offer different opportunities for good and bad behavior, for virtue and vice, for justice and injustice, but those standards govern human behavior, not endowments or outcomes. The equal application of standards is the moral realization of morally equal status, on the basis of which we may morally judge behavior. Moral equality means that a crime is a crime, regardless of whether committed by a taxi driver or a tycoon, and an honest trade resulting in profit is an honest trade, regardless of whether undertaken by two taxi drivers, by two tycoons, or by a tycoon and a taxi driver.

Let's return to the consideration of the relationship of wealth and equality. Wealth holdings can be the results of either just behavior or of coercion. Free market exchanges can result in either greater inequality or greater equality, and state interventions and redistributions can also result in either greater inequality or greater equality. There is nothing inherently equal or unequal about either kind of interaction. An entrepreneur can create wealth and thus have more than another person, even if the wealth creation benefited that other person, as well. Exchanges in free markets may also result in greater equality, through generating widespread prosperity and through eroding the unjust privileges of the powerful that were inherited from previous systems. A robber can steal from someone and then have more than the victim, resulting in greater inequality, or the same as the victim, resulting in greater equality. Similarly, interventions by the organized coercive power of the state may result in enormous inequalities of wealth, either through overriding choices made by market participants (through protectionism, subsidies, and "rent-seeking") or merely through the exercise of brutal force and violence, as certainly happened in countries under communist rule. (Being officially dedicated to equality is not the same as actually producing equality, as bitter experience over decades showed.)

Whether a legal and economic system produces greater or lesser approximations to equality of income, for example, is an empirical matter, not a conceptual one. *The Economic Freedom of the World Report* (www.freetheworld.com) measures degrees of economic freedom and then compares the indices to a variety of indicators of economic well being (longevity, literacy, degree of corruption, per capita income, etc.). The data show not only that residents of countries with the freest economies are much wealthier than those with less economic freedom, but also that inequality of income (specifically, the share of national income earned by the poorest 10% of the population) is not a feature of different policies, whereas the amount of income they earn is. Considering the countries of the world by quartiles (each with 25% of the world's countries) the average share of national income going to the poorest 10% of the population in the least-free quartile (including such countries as Zimbabwe, Myanmar, and Syria) in 2008 (the last year for which data are available) was 2.47%; in the next (third most-free) quartile, 2.19%; in the next (second most-free) quartile, 2.27%; and in the freest quartile, 2.58%. The variation is hardly significant. That is to say, such inequality seems to be immune to being affected by the rules of economic policies. On the other hand, the amount of income the poorest 10% receive varies enormously, precisely because that variable is certainly not immune to economic policies. Being among the poorest 10% in the least-free countries means an average annual income of $910 per year, while being among the poorest 10% in the most-free market economies means an average annual income of $8,474. For those who are poor, it seems far better to be poor in Switzerland than in Syria.

Whether you and I have equal initial endowments before free exchanges or equal holdings after free exchanges is not, by itself, a moral problem. On the other hand, refusing to treat morally equal persons equally and to apply equal rules to them, all in the attempt to generate more equal outcomes (not, it seems, a generally successful enterprise, as such outcomes are not so easily manipulated), certainly *is* a moral problem. That is a violation of moral equality that matters.

The biggest scandal in the world regarding inequality of wealth is not the inequality between the wealthy and the poor in economically free societies, but that huge gap between the wealth of people in economically free societies and the wealth of people in economically unfree societies. That gap between wealth and poverty is quite certainly a matter that can be solved by changing the rules, i.e., by changing economic policies. Freeing the people of economically unfree societies will create enormous amounts of wealth that would do more to narrow the gap between the world's wealthy and the world's poor than any other policy imaginable. Moreover, it would do so as a positive consequence of the realization of justice, by eliminating the unequal treatment of people in countries misruled through cronyism, statism, militarism, socialism, corruption, and brute force. Economic freedom, that is, equal standards of justice and equal respect for the rights of all to produce and to exchange, is the right standard of justice for moral beings.

Adam Smith and the Myth of Greed

By Tom G. Palmer

In this essay, the author lays to rest the myth of a naïve Adam Smith who believed that merely relying on "self interest" would create prosperity. Those who cite Smith to that effect have not, it seems, ever read more than a few quotations from his works and are unaware of the great emphasis he put on the role of institutions and on the harmful effects of self-interested behavior when channeled through the coercive institutions of the state. The rule of law, property, contract, and exchange channel self-interest into mutual benefit, whereas lawlessness and disrespect for property give self-interest an altogether different and profoundly harmful outlet.

One frequently hears it said that Adam Smith believed that if people were only to act selfishly, all would go well in the world, that "Greed makes the world go round." Smith, of course, did not believe that relying exclusively on selfish motivations would make the world a better place, nor did he promote or encourage selfish behavior. His extensive discussion in *The Theory of Moral Sentiments* of the role of the "impartial spectator" should put such misinterpretations to rest. Smith was not an advocate of selfishness, but he was also not naïve enough to think that selfless devotion to the welfare of others (or professing such devotion) would make the world better, either. As Steven Holmes noted in his corrective essay "The Secret History of Self-Interest,"[32] Smith knew very well the destructive effects of many "disinterested" passions, such as envy, malice, revenge, zealotry, and the like. The selfless zealots of the Spanish Inquisition did what they did in the hope that in the last moment of agony the dying heretics might repent and receive God's grace. That was known as the doctrine of salvific justification. Humbert de Romans, in his instruction to inquisitors, insisted that they justify to the congregation the punishments to be imposed on heretics, for "We beg God, and we beg you, that you should beg him together with me, that from the gift of his grace he should make it that those to be punished bear so patiently the punishments that we propose to impose upon them (in the demand of justice, nevertheless with grief), that it might redound to their salvation. Because of this we impose such a punishment."[33] In Smith's view, such selfless devotion to the welfare of others was not obviously morally superior to the allegedly selfish merchants seeking to enrich themselves by selling ale and salted fish to thirsty and hungry customers.

Smith is hardly a general endorser of selfish behavior, for whether such motivations lead "as if by an invisible hand" to the promotion of the general good depends very much on the context of the actions, and particularly on the institutional setting.

Sometimes the self-centered desire to be liked by others can indeed lead one to adopt a moral perspective, by causing us to think about how we appear to others. In the kind of small-scale interpersonal settings typically described in *The Theory of Moral Sentiments*, such motivation may redound to the general benefit, for the "desire to become ourselves the objects of the like agreeable sentiments, and to be as amiable and as admirable as those whom we love and admire the most" requires us to "become the impartial spectators of our own character and conduct."[34] Even apparently excessive self-interest, when in the right institutional setting, can be to the benefit of others, such as in the story Smith tells of the poor man's son whose ambition causes him to work tirelessly to accumulate wealth, only to find after a lifetime of hard work that he is no happier than the simple beggar sunning himself on the side of the road; the ambitiously excessive pursuit of self-interest on the part of the poor man's son benefited the rest of humanity by leading him to produce and accumulate the wealth that made the very existence of many others possible, for "the earth by these labours of mankind has been obliged to redouble her natural fertility, and to maintain a greater multitude of inhabitants."[35]

In the larger context of political economy described in many passages of *An Inquiry into the Nature and Causes of the Wealth of Nations*, specifically those involving interaction with the institutions of the state, the pursuit of self-interest is not so likely to have positive effects. The self-interest of merchants, for example, leads them to lobby the state to create cartels, protectionism, and even war: "to expect, indeed, that the freedom of trade should ever be entirely restored in Great Britain, is as absurd as to expect that an Oceana or Utopia should ever be established in it. Not only the prejudices of the publick, but what is much more unconquerable, the private interests of many individuals, irresistibly oppose it."[36] The trifling gains of merchants from monopolies are purchased at the expense of horrific burdens to the public in the case of empires and wars:

> [I]n the system of laws which has been established for the management of our American and West Indian colonies, the interest of the home-consumer has been sacrificed to that of the producer with a more extravagant profusion than in all our other commercial regulations. A great empire has been established for the sole purpose of raising up a nation of customers who should be obliged to buy from the shops of our different producers, all the goods with which these could supply them. For the sake of that little enhancement of price which this monopoly might afford our producers, the home-consumers have been burdened with the whole expense of maintaining and defending that empire. For this purpose, and for this purpose only, in the two last wars, more than two hundred millions have been spent, and a new debt of more than a hundred and seventy millions has been contracted over and above all that had been expended for the same purpose in former wars. The interest of this debt alone is not only greater than the whole extraordinary profit, which, it ever could be pretended, was made by the monopoly of the colony trade, but than the whole value of that trade or than that whole value of the goods, which at an average have been annually exported to the colonies.[37]

So Smith's views on whether, in the words of Gordon Gecko, the fictional character from Oliver Stone's film *Wall Street*, "Greed is good" is decidedly "sometimes yes, and sometimes no" (assuming that all self-interested behavior is "greed"). The difference is in the institutional setting.

What about the common view that markets promote selfish behavior, that the psychological attitude engendered by exchange encourages selfishness? I know of no good reason to think that markets promote selfishness or greed, in the sense that market interaction increases the quantum of greediness or the propensity of people to be selfish, over what is observed in societies governed by states that suppress or discourage or interfere in or disrupt markets. In fact, markets make it possible for the most altruistic, as well as the most selfish, to advance their purposes in peace. Those who dedicate their lives to helping others use markets to advance their purposes, no less than those whose goal is to increase their store of wealth. Some of the latter even accumulate wealth for the purpose of increasing their ability to help others. George Soros and Bill Gates are examples of the latter; they earn huge amounts of money, at least partly in order to increase their ability to help others through their vast charitable activities. The creation of wealth in the pursuit of profits enables them to be generous.

A philanthropist or saint wants to use the wealth available to her to feed, clothe, and comfort the greatest number of people. Markets allow her to find the lowest prices for blankets, for food, and for medicines to care for those who need her assistance. Markets allow the creation of wealth that can be used to help the unfortunate and facilitate the charitable to maximize their ability to help others. Markets make possible the charity of the charitable.

A common mistake is to identify the purposes of people exclusively with their "self-interest," which is then in turn confused with "selfishness." The purposes of people in the market are indeed purposes of selves, but as selves with purposes we are also concerned about the interests and well being of others—our family members, our friends, our neighbors, and even total strangers whom we will never meet. Indeed, markets help to condition people to consider the needs of others, including total strangers.

Philip Wicksteed offered a nuanced treatment of motivations in market exchanges. Rather than using "selfishness" to describe the motivations for engaging in market exchanges (one might go to the market to buy food for the poor, for example), he coined the term "non-tuism."[38] We might sell our products to gain money to be able to help out our friends, or even distant strangers, but when we haggle for the lowest or highest price, we rarely do so out of a concern for the well being of the party with whom we're bargaining. If we do, we are making an exchange and a gift, which somewhat complicates the nature of the exchange. Those who deliberately pay more than they need to are rarely good businesspeople and, as H.B. Acton noted in his book *The Morals of the Markets*,[39] running a business at a loss is in general a very foolish, even stupid, way to be philanthropic.

To those who praise involvement in politics over involvement in industry and commerce, it is worth remembering that the former can do a great deal of harm and rarely does much good. Voltaire, writing before Smith, saw the difference clearly. In his essay "On Trade" from his *Letters Concerning the English Nation* (written by Voltaire in English, in which he was quite fluent, and then rewritten by him in French and published as *Lettres Philosophiques*) he noted that,

> In *France* the Title of Marquis is given gratis to any one who will accept of it; and whosoever arrives at Paris from the midst of the most remote Provinces with Money in his Purse, and a Name terminating in *ac* or *ille*, may strut about, and cry, Such a Man as I! A Man of my Rank and Figure! And may look down upon a Trader with sovereign Contempt; whilst the Trader on the other Side, by thus often hearing his Profession treated so disdainfully, is Fool enough to blush at it. However, I cannot say which is most useful to a Nation; a Lord, powder'd in the tip of the Mode, who knows exactly at what a Clock the King rises and goes to bed; and who gives himself Airs of Grandeur and State, at the same Time that he is acting the Slave in the Anti-chamber of a prime Minister; or a Merchant, who enriches his Country, dispatches Orders from his Compting-House to *Surat* and *Grand Cairo*, and contributes to the felicity of the world.[40]

Merchants and capitalists need not blush when our contemporary politicians and intellectuals look down their noses at them, and strut about declaiming this and decrying that, all the while demanding that the merchants, capitalists, workers, investors, craftsmen, farmers, inventors, and other productive producers create the wealth that the politicians confiscate and the anti-capitalistic intellectuals resent but greedily consume.

Markets do not depend on or presuppose people being selfish, any more than politics does. Nor do market exchanges encourage more selfish behavior or motivation. But unlike politics, free exchange among willing participants does generate wealth and peace, which are conditions under which generosity, friendship, and love flourish. There is something to be said for that, as Adam Smith well understood.

Ayn Rand and Capitalism: The Moral Revolution

By David Kelley

In this essay, the Objectivist philosopher David Kelley proposes a "fourth revolution" to complete the foundations of the modern world and to secure the gains made possible by capitalism.

David Kelley is executive director of The Atlas Society, which promotes the development and dissemination of the philosophy of Objectivism. Kelley is the author of The Evidence of the Senses, The Art of Reasoning *(one of the most widely used textbooks on logic in the United States),* A Life of One's Own: Individual Rights and the Welfare State, *and other books. He taught philosophy at Vassar College and Brandeis University and has published widely in the popular press, including such publications as* Harper's, The Sciences, Reason, Harvard Business Review, *and* Barron's.

This essay is reprinted by permission of the author from The New Individualist, *spring 2009.*

"We have it in our power to begin the world over again."
—Thomas Paine, *Common Sense*, 1792.

The crisis in financial markets has set off a predictable torrent of anti-capitalist sentiment. Despite the fact that government regulations were a major cause of the crisis, anti-capitalists and their enablers in the media have blamed the market and called for new restraints. The government has already exerted an unprecedented degree of intervention in financial markets, and it now seems clear that new economic controls will expand far beyond Wall Street.

Regulation of production and trade is one of the two basic things that government does in our mixed economy. The other is redistribution—transferring income and wealth from one set of hands to another. In this realm, too, anti-capitalists have seized the moment to call for new entitlements such as guaranteed health care, along with new tax burdens on the wealthy. The economic crisis, along with the election of Barack Obama, has revealed a huge pent-up demand for redistribution. Where does that demand come from? To answer that question in fundamental terms, we need to look back at the origins of capitalism and look more closely at the arguments for redistribution.

The capitalist system came of age in the century from 1750 to 1850 as a result of three revolutions. The first was a political revolution: the triumph of liberalism, particularly the doctrine of natural rights, and the view that government should be limited in its function to the protection of individual rights, including property rights. The second revolution was the birth of economic understanding, exemplified by Adam Smith's *Wealth of Nations*. Smith demonstrated that when individuals are left free to pursue their own economic interests, the result is not chaos but a spontaneous order, a market system in which the actions of individuals are coordinated and more wealth is produced than would be the case if government managed the economy. The third revolution was, of course, the Industrial Revolution. Technological innovation provided a lever that vastly multiplied man's powers of production. The effect was not only to raise standards of living for everyone, but to offer the alert and enterprising individual the prospect of earning a fortune unimaginable in earlier times.

The political revolution, the triumph of the doctrine of individual rights, was accompanied by a spirit of moral idealism. It was the liberation of man from tyranny, the recognition that every individual, whatever his station in society, is an end in himself. But the economic revolution was couched in morally ambiguous terms: as an economic system, capitalism was widely regarded as having been conceived in sin. The desire for wealth fell under the shadow of the Christian injunction against selfishness and avarice. The early students of spontaneous order were conscious that they were asserting a moral paradox—the paradox, as Bernard Mandeville put it, that private vices could produce public benefits.

The critics of the market have always capitalized on these doubts about its morality. The socialist movement was sustained by allegations that capitalism breeds selfishness, exploitation, alienation, injustice. In milder forms, this same belief produced the welfare state, which redistributes income through government programs in the name of "social justice." Capitalism has never escaped the moral ambiguity in which it was conceived. It is valued for the prosperity it brings; it is valued as a necessary precondition for political and intellectual freedom. But few of its defenders are prepared to assert that the mode of life central to capitalism—the pursuit of self-interest through production and trade—is morally honorable, much less noble or ideal.

There is no mystery about where the moral antipathy toward the market comes from. It arises from the ethics of altruism, which is deeply rooted in Western culture, as indeed in most cultures. By the standards of altruism, the pursuit of self-interest is at best a neutral act, outside the realm of morality, and at worst a sin. It is true that success in the market is achieved by voluntary trade, and thus by satisfying the needs of others. But it is also true that those who do succeed are motivated by personal gain, and ethics is as much concerned with motives as with results.

In everyday speech, the term "altruism" is often taken to mean nothing more than kindness or common courtesy. But its real meaning, historically and philosophically, is self-sacrifice. For the socialists who coined the term, it meant the complete submersion of the self in a larger social whole. As Ayn Rand put it, "The basic principle of altruism is that man has no right to exist for his own sake, that service to others is the only justification of his existence, and that self-sacrifice is his highest moral duty, virtue, and value." Altruism in this strict sense is the basis for the various concepts of "social justice" that are used to defend government programs for redistributing wealth. Those programs represent the compulsory sacrifice of the people taxed to support them. They represent the use of individuals as collective resources, to be used as means to the ends of others. And that is the fundamental reason why they should be opposed on moral grounds by anyone who defends capitalism.

Demands for Social Justice

Demands for social justice take two different forms, which I will call welfarism and egalitarianism. According to welfarism, individuals have a right to certain necessities of life, including minimum levels of food, shelter, clothing, medical care, education, and so on. It is the responsibility of society to ensure that all members have access to these necessities. But a laissez-faire capitalist system does not guarantee them to everyone. Thus, argue the welfarists, capitalism fails to satisfy its moral responsibility and so must be modified through state action to provide such goods to people who cannot obtain them by their own efforts.

According to egalitarianism, the wealth produced by a society must be distributed fairly. It is unjust for some people to earn fifteen, or fifty, or a hundred times as much income as others. But laissez-faire capitalism permits and encourages these disparities in income and wealth, and is therefore unjust. The hallmark of egalitarianism is the use of statistics on the distribution of income. In 2007, for example, the top 20 percent of United States households on the income scale earned 50 percent of total income, whereas the bottom 20 percent earned only 3.4 percent. The goal of egalitarianism is to reduce this difference; any change in the direction of greater equality is regarded as a gain in equity.

The difference in these two conceptions of social justice is the difference between absolute and relative levels of well-being. The welfarist demands that people have access to a certain minimum standard of living. As long as this floor or "safety net" exists, it does not matter how much wealth anyone else has, or how great the disparities are between rich and poor. So welfarists are primarily interested in programs that benefit people who are below a certain level of poverty, or who are sick, out of work, or deprived in some other way. Egalitarians, on the other hand, are concerned with *relative* well-being. Egalitarians have often said that of two societies, they prefer the one in which wealth is more evenly distributed, even if its overall standard of living is lower. Thus, egalitarians tend to favor government measures such as progressive taxation, which aim to redistribute wealth across the entire income scale, not merely at the bottom. They also tend to support the nationalization of goods such as education and medicine, taking them off the market entirely and making them available to everyone more or less equally.

Let us consider these two concepts of social justice in turn.

Welfarism: The Unchosen Obligation

The fundamental premise of welfarism is that people have rights to goods such as food, shelter, and medical care. They are *entitled* to these things. On this assumption, someone who receives benefits from a government program is merely getting what is due him, in the same way that a buyer who receives the good he has paid for is merely getting his due. When the state dispenses welfare benefits, it is merely protecting rights, just as it is when it protects a buyer against fraud. In neither case is there any necessity for gratitude.

The concept of welfare rights, or positive rights as they are often called, is modeled on the traditional liberal rights of life, liberty, and property. But there is a well-known difference. The traditional rights are rights to act without interference from others. The right to life is a right to act with the aim of preserving oneself. It is not a right to be immune from death by natural causes, even an untimely death. The right to property is the right to buy and sell freely, and to appropriate unowned goods from nature. It is the right to seek property, but not a right to a dowry from nature, or from the state; it is not a guarantee that one will succeed in acquiring anything. Accordingly, these rights impose on other people only the negative obligation not to interfere, not to restrain one forcibly from acting as he chooses. If I imagine myself removed from society—living on a desert island, for example—my rights would be perfectly secure. I might not live long, and certainly would not live well, but I would live in perfect freedom from murder, theft, and assault.

By contrast, welfare rights are conceived as rights to possess and enjoy certain goods, regardless of one's actions; they are rights to have the goods provided by others if one cannot earn them oneself. Accordingly, welfare rights impose positive obligations on others. If I have a right to food, someone has an obligation to grow it. If I cannot pay for it, someone has an obligation to buy it for me. Welfarists sometimes argue that the obligation is imposed on society as a whole, not on any specific individual. But society is not an entity, much less a moral agent, over and above its individual members, so any such obligation falls upon us as individuals. Insofar as welfare rights are implemented through government programs, for example, the obligation is distributed over all taxpayers.

From an ethical standpoint, then, the essence of welfarism is the premise that the need of one individual is a claim on other individuals. The claim may run only as far as the town or the nation. It may not embrace all of humanity. But in all versions of the doctrine, the claim does not depend on your personal relationship to the claimant, or your choice to help, or your evaluation of him as worthy of your help. It is an unchosen obligation arising from the sheer fact of his need.

But we must carry the analysis one step further. If I am living alone on a desert island, then of course I have no welfare rights, since there is no one else around to provide the goods. For the same reason, if I live in a primitive society where medicine is unknown, then I have no right to medical care. The content of welfare rights is relative to the level of economic wealth and productive capacity in a given society. Correspondingly, the obligation of individuals to satisfy the needs of others is dependent on their ability to do so. I cannot be blamed as an individual for failing to provide others with something I cannot produce for myself.

Suppose I can produce it and simply choose not to? Suppose I am capable of earning a much larger income than I do, the taxes on which would support a person who will otherwise go hungry. Am I obliged to work harder, to earn more, for the sake of that person? I do not know any philosopher of welfare who would say that I am. The moral claim imposed on me by another person's need is contingent not only on my ability but also on my *willingness* to produce.

And this tells us something important about the ethical focus of welfarism. It does not assert an obligation to pursue the satisfaction of human needs, much less the obligation to succeed in doing so. The obligation, rather, is conditional: those who do succeed in creating wealth may do so only on condition that others are allowed to share the wealth. The goal is not so much to benefit the needy as to bind the able. The implicit assumption is that a person's ability and initiative are social assets, which may be exercised only on condition that they are aimed at the service of others.

Egalitarianism: "Fair" Distribution

If we turn to egalitarianism, we find that we arrive at the same principle by a different logical route. The ethical framework of the egalitarian is defined by the concept of justice rather than rights. If we look at society as a whole, we see that income, wealth, and power are distributed in a certain way among individuals and groups. The basic question is: is the existing distribution fair? If not, then it must be corrected by government programs of redistribution. A pure market economy, of course, does not produce equality among individuals. But few egalitarians have claimed that strict equality of outcome is required by justice. The most common position is that there is a presumption in favor of equal outcomes, and that any departure from equality must be justified by its benefits to society as a whole. Thus, the English writer R. H. Tawney wrote that "inequality of circumstance is regarded as reasonable, in so far as it is a necessary condition of securing the services which the community requires." John Rawls's famous "Difference Principle"—that inequalities are permitted as long as they serve the interests of the least advantaged persons in society—is only the most recent example of this approach. In other words, egalitarians recognize that strict leveling would have a disastrous effect on production. They admit that not everyone contributes equally to the wealth of a society. To some extent, therefore, people must be rewarded in accordance with their productive ability, as an incentive to put forth their best efforts. But any such differences must be limited to those which are necessary for the public good.

What is the philosophical basis of this principle? Egalitarians often argue that it follows logically from the basic principle of justice: that people are to be treated differently only if they differ in some morally relevant way. If we are going to apply this fundamental principle to the distribution of income, however, we must first assume that society literally engages in an act of distributing income. This assumption is plainly false. In a market economy, incomes are determined by the choices of millions of individuals—consumers, investors, entrepreneurs, and workers. These choices are coordinated by the laws of supply and demand,

and it is no accident that a successful entrepreneur, say, earns much more than a day laborer. But this is not the result of any conscious intention on the part of society. In 2007 the most highly paid entertainer in the United States was Oprah Winfrey, who earned some $260 million. This was not because "society" decided she was worth that much, but because millions of fans decided that her show was worth watching. Even in a socialist economy, as we now know, economic outcomes are not under the control of government planners. Even here there is a spontaneous order, albeit a corrupt one, in which outcomes are determined by bureaucratic infighting, black markets, and so forth.

Despite the absence of any literal act of distribution, egalitarians often argue that society is responsible for ensuring that the statistical distribution of income meets certain standards of fairness. Why? Because the production of wealth is a cooperative, social process. More wealth is created in a society characterized by trade and the division of labor than in a society of self-sufficient producers. The division of labor means that many people contribute to the final product; and trade means that an even wider circle of people share responsibility for the wealth that is obtained by the producers. Production is so transformed by these relationships, say the egalitarians, that the group as a whole must be considered the real unit of production and the real source of wealth. At least it is the source of the difference in wealth that exists between a cooperative and a non-cooperative society. Therefore society must ensure that the fruits of cooperation are fairly distributed among all participants.

But this argument is valid only if we regard economic wealth as an anonymous social product in which it is impossible to isolate individual contributions. Only in that case will it be necessary to devise after-the-fact principles of distributive justice for allocating shares of the product. But this assumption, once again, is plainly wrong. The so-called social product is actually a vast array of individual goods and services available on the market. It is certainly possible to know which good or service any individual has helped to produce. And when the product is produced by a group of individuals, as in a firm, it is possible to identify who did what. After all, an employer does not hire workers by whim.

A worker is hired because of the anticipated difference his efforts will make to the final product. This fact is acknowledged by the egalitarians themselves when they allow that inequalities are acceptable if they are an incentive for the more productive to increase the total wealth of a society. To ensure that the incentives are going to the right people, as Robert Nozick has observed, even the egalitarian must assume that we can identify the role of individual contributions. In short, there is no basis for applying the concept of justice to the statistical distributions of income or wealth across an entire economy. We must abandon the picture of a large pie that is being divided up by a benevolent parent who wishes to be fair to all the children at the table.

Once we abandon this picture, what becomes of the principle espoused by Tawney, Rawls, and others: the principle that inequalities are acceptable only if they serve the interests of all? If this cannot be grounded in justice, then it must be regarded as a matter of the obligations we bear to each other as individuals. When we consider it in this light, we can see that it is the same principle we identified as the basis of welfare rights. The principle is that the productive may enjoy the fruits of their efforts only on condition that their efforts benefit others as well. There is no obligation to produce, to create, to earn an income. But if you do, the needs of others arise as a constraint on your actions. Your ability, your initiative, your intelligence, your dedication to your goals, and all the other qualities that make success possible, are personal assets that put you under an obligation to those with less ability, initiative, intelligence, or dedication.

In other words, every form of social justice rests on the assumption that individual ability is a social asset. The assumption is not merely that the individual may not use his talents to trample on the rights of the less able. Nor does the assumption say merely that kindness or generosity are virtues. It says that the individual must regard himself, in part at least, as a means to the good of others. And here we come to the crux of the matter. In respecting the rights of other people, I recognize that they are ends in themselves, that I may not treat them merely as means to my satisfaction, in the way that I treat inanimate objects. Why then is it not equally moral to regard myself as an end? Why should

I not refuse, out of respect for my own dignity as a moral being, to regard myself as a means in the service of others?

Toward an Individualist Ethics

Ayn Rand's case for capitalism rests on an individualist ethics that recognizes the moral right to pursue one's self-interest and rejects altruism at the root.

Altruists argue that life presents us with a basic choice: we must either sacrifice others to ourselves, or sacrifice ourselves to others. The latter is the altruist course of action, and the assumption is that the only alternative is life as a predator. But this is a false alternative, according to Rand. Life does not require sacrifices in either direction. The interests of rational people do not conflict, and the pursuit of our genuine self-interest requires that we deal with others by means of peaceful, voluntary exchange.

To see why, let us ask how we decide what is in our self-interest. An interest is a value that we seek to obtain: wealth, pleasure, security, love, self-esteem, or some other good. Rand's ethical philosophy is based on the insight that the fundamental value, the *summum bonum*, is life. It is the existence of living organisms, their need to maintain themselves through constant action to satisfy their needs that gives rise to the entire phenomenon of values. A world without life would be a world of facts but not values, a world in which no state could be said to be better or worse than any other. Thus the fundamental standard of value, by reference to which a person must judge what is in his interest, is his life: not mere survival from one moment to another, but the full satisfaction of his needs through the ongoing exercise of his faculties.

Man's primary faculty, his primary means of survival, is his capacity for reason. It is reason that allows us to live by production, and thus to rise above the precarious level of hunting and gathering. Reason is the basis of language, which makes it possible for us to cooperate and transmit knowledge. Reason is the basis of social institutions governed by abstract rules. The purpose of ethics is to provide standards for living in accordance with reason, in the service of our lives.

To live by reason we must accept independence as a virtue. Reason is a faculty of the individual. No matter how much we learn from others, the act of thought takes place in the individual mind. It must be initiated by each of us by our own choice and directed by our own mental effort. Rationality therefore requires that we accept responsibility for directing and sustaining our own lives.

To live by reason, we must also accept productiveness as a virtue. Production is the act of creating value. Human beings cannot live secure and fulfilling lives by finding what they need in nature, as other animals do. Nor can they live as parasites on others. "If some men attempt to survive by means of brute force or fraud," argues Rand, "by looting, robbing, cheating or enslaving the men who produce, it still remains true that their survival is made possible only by their victims, only by the men who choose to think and to produce the goods which they, the looters, are seizing. Such looters are parasites incapable of survival, who exist by destroying those who are capable, those who are pursuing a course of action proper to man."

The egoist is usually pictured as someone who will do anything to get what he wants—someone who will lie, steal, and seek to dominate others in order to satisfy his desires. Like most people, Rand would regard this mode of life as immoral. But her reason is not that it harms others. Her reason is that it harms the self. Subjective desire is not the test for whether something is in our interest, and deceit, theft, and power are not the means for achieving happiness or a successful life. The virtues I've mentioned are objective standards. They are rooted in man's nature, and thus apply to all human beings. But their purpose is to enable each person to "achieve, maintain, fulfill, and enjoy that ultimate value, that end in itself, which is his own life." Thus the purpose of ethics is to tell us how to achieve our real interests, not how to sacrifice them.

The Trader Principle

How then should we deal with others? Rand's social ethics rests on two basic principles: a principle of rights and a principle of justice. The principle of rights says that we must deal with others peaceably, by voluntary exchange, without initiating the use of force against them. It is only in this way that we can live independently, on the basis of our own productive efforts; the person who attempts to live by controlling others is a parasite. Within an organized society, moreover, we must respect the rights of others if we wish our own rights to be respected. And it is only in this way that we can obtain the many benefits that come from social interaction: the benefits of economic and intellectual exchange, as well as the values of more intimate personal relationships. The source of these benefits is the rationality, the productiveness, the individuality of the other person, and these things require freedom to flourish. If I live by force, I attack the root of the values I seek.

The principle of justice is what Rand calls the trader principle: living by trade, offering value for value, neither seeking nor granting the unearned. An honorable person does not offer his needs as a claim on others; he offers value as the basis of any relationship. Nor does he accept an unchosen obligation to serve the needs of others. No one who values his own life can accept an open-ended responsibility to be his brother's keeper. Nor would an independent person wish to be kept—not by a master, and not by the Department of Health and Human Services. The principle of trade, Rand observes, is the only basis on which humans can deal with each other as independent equals.

The Objectivist ethics, in short, treats the individual as an end in himself in the full meaning of that term. The implication is that capitalism is the only just and moral system. A capitalist society is based on the recognition and protection of individual rights. In a capitalist society, men are free to pursue their own ends, by the exercise of their own minds. As in any society, men are constrained by the laws of nature. Food, shelter, clothing, books, and medicine do not grow on trees; they must be produced. And as in any society, men also are constrained by the limitations of their own nature, the extent of their individual ability. But the only social constraint that capitalism imposes is the requirement that those who wish the services of others must offer value in return. No one may use the state to expropriate what others have produced.

Economic outcomes in the market—the distribution of income and wealth—depend on the voluntary actions and interactions of all the participants. The concept of justice applies not to the outcome but to the process of economic activity. A person's income is just if it is won through voluntary exchange, as a reward for value offered, as judged by those to whom it is offered. Economists have long known that there is no such thing as a just price for a good, apart from the judgments of market participants about the value of the good to them. The same is true for the price of human productive services. This is not to say that I must measure my worth by my income, but only that if I wish to live by trade with others, I cannot demand that they accept my terms at the sacrifice of their own self-interest.

Benevolence as a Chosen Value

What about someone who is poor, disabled, or otherwise unable to support himself? This is a valid question to ask, as long as it is not the first question we ask about a social system. It is a legacy of altruism to think that the primary standard by which to evaluate a society is the way it treats its least productive members. "Blessed are the poor in spirit," said Jesus; "blessed are the meek." But there is no ground in justice for holding the poor or the meek in any special esteem or regarding their needs as primary. If we had to choose between a collectivist society in which no one is free but no one is hungry, and an individualist society in which everyone is free but a few people starve, I would argue that the second society, the free one, is the moral choice. No one can claim a right to make others serve him involuntarily, even if his own life depends on it.

But this is not the choice we face. In fact, the poor are much better off under capitalism than under socialism, or even the welfare state. As a matter of historical fact, the societies in which no one is free, like the former Soviet Union, are societies in which large numbers of people go hungry.

Those who are capable of working at all have a vital interest in economic and technological growth, which occur most rapidly in a market order. The investment of capital and the use of machinery make it possible to employ people who otherwise could not produce enough to support themselves. Computers and communications equipment, for example, have now made it possible for severely disabled people to work from their homes.

As for those who simply cannot work, free societies have always provided numerous forms of private aid and philanthropy outside the market: charitable organizations, benevolent societies, and the like. In this regard, let us be clear that there is no contradiction between egoism and charity. In light of the many benefits we receive from dealing with others, it is natural to regard our fellow humans in a spirit of general benevolence, to sympathize with their misfortunes, and to give aid when it does not require a sacrifice of our own interests. But there are major differences between an egoist and an altruist conception of charity.

For an altruist, generosity to others is an ethical primary, and it should be carried to the point of sacrifice, on the principle "give until it hurts." It is a moral duty to give, regardless of any other values one has, and the recipient has a right to it. For an egoist, generosity is one among many means of pursuing our values, including the value that we place on the well-being of others. It should be done in the context of one's other values, on the principle "give when it helps." It is not a duty, nor do the recipients have a right to it. An altruist tends to regard generosity as an expiation of guilt, on the assumption that there is something sinful or suspicious about being able, successful, productive, or wealthy. An egoist regards those same traits as virtues and sees generosity as an expression of pride in them.

The Fourth Revolution

I said at the outset that capitalism was the result of three revolutions, each of them a radical break with the past. The political revolution established the primacy of individual rights and the principle that government is man's servant, not his master. The economic revolution brought an understanding of markets. The Industrial Revolution radically expanded the application of intelligence to the process of production. But mankind never broke with its ethical past. The ethical principle that individual ability is a social asset is incompatible with a free society. If freedom is to survive and flourish, we need a fourth revolution, a moral revolution, that establishes the moral right of the individual to live for himself.

Section III

The Production and Distribution of Wealth

The Market Economy and the Distribution of Wealth

By Ludwig Lachmann

In this essay, the distinguished economist Ludwig Lachmann examines the "social justice" critiques of free-market capitalism and reveals their incoherence. He explains the difference between "ownership" and "wealth" and shows how respect for property (ownership) is compatible with massive redistribution of wealth through the market. This essay is important for understanding the dynamic nature of social and economic relations in capitalist orders.

Ludwig Lachmann (1906–1990) received his Ph.D. at the University of Berlin. He left Germany in 1933 for England, where he continued his research at the London School of Economics. Lachmann made substantial contributions to the theory of capital, economic growth, and the methodological foundations of economics and sociology. He was the author of such books as Capital and Its Structure; The Legacy of Max Weber; Macro-Economic Thinking and the Market Economy; Capital, Expectations, and the Market Process; *and* The Market as an Economic Process.

This essay is a slightly abridged version of the original, which first appeared in 1956.

Who can now doubt that, as Professor Mises pointed out thirty years ago, every intervention by a political authority entails a further intervention to prevent the inevitable economic repercussions of the first step from taking place? Who will deny that a command economy requires an atmosphere of inflation to operate at all, and who today does not know the baneful effects of "controlled inflation"? Even though some economists have now invented the eulogistic term "secular inflation" in order to describe the permanent inflation we all know so well, it is unlikely that anyone is deceived. It did not really require the recent German example to demonstrate to us that a market economy will create order out of "administratively controlled" chaos even in the most unfavorable circumstances. A form of economic organization based on voluntary cooperation and the universal exchange of knowledge is necessarily superior to any hierarchical structure, even if in the latter a rational test for the qualifications of those who give the word of command could exist. Those who are able to learn from reason and experience knew it before, and those who are not are unlikely to learn it even now.

Confronted with this situation, the opponents of the market economy have shifted their ground; they now oppose it on "social" rather than economic grounds. They accuse it of being unjust rather than inefficient. They now dwell on the "distorting effects" of the ownership of wealth and contend that "the plebiscite of the market is swayed by plural voting." They show that the distribution of wealth affects production and income distribution since the owners of wealth not merely receive an "unfair share" of the social income, but will also influence the composition of the social product: luxuries are too many and necessities too few. Moreover, since these owners do most of the saving, they also determine the rate of capital accumulation and thus of economic progress.

Some of these opponents would not altogether deny that there is a sense in which the distribution of wealth is the cumulative result of the play of economic forces, but would hold that this accumulation operates in such a fashion as to make the present a slave of the past, a bygone and arbitrary factor in the present. Today's income distribution is shaped by today's distribution of wealth, and even though today's wealth was partly accumulated yesterday, it was accumulated by processes reflecting the influence of the distribution of wealth on the day before yesterday. In the main this argument of the opponents of the market economy is based on the institution of "inheritance" to which, even in a progressive society, we are told, a majority of the owners owe their wealth.

This argument appears to be widely accepted today, even by many who are genuinely in favor of economic freedom. Such people have come to believe that a "redistribution of wealth," for instance through death duties, would have socially desirable, but no unfavorable, economic results. On the contrary, since such measures would help to free the present from the "dead hand" of the past they would also help to adjust present incomes to present needs. The distribution of wealth is a datum of the market, and by changing data we can change results without interfering with the market mechanism! It follows that only when accompanied by a policy designed continually to redistribute existing wealth, would the market process have "socially tolerable" results.

This view, as we said, is today held by many, even by some economists who understand the superiority of the market economy over the command economy and the frustrations of interventionism, but dislike what they regard as the social consequences of the market economy. They are prepared to accept the market economy only where its operation is accompanied by such a policy of redistribution.

The present paper is devoted to a criticism of the basis of this view.

In the first place, the whole argument rests logically on verbal confusion arising from the ambiguous meaning of the term "datum." In common usage as well as in most sciences, for instance in statistics, the word "datum" means something that is, at a moment of time, "given" to us as observers of the scene. In this sense it is, of course, a truism that the mode of the distribution of wealth is a datum at any given moment of time, simply in the trivial sense that it happens to exist and no other mode does. But in the equilibrium theories that, for better or worse, have come to mean so much for present-day economic thought and have so largely shaped its content, the word "datum" has acquired a second and very different meaning: Here a datum means a necessary condition of equilibrium, an independent variable, and "the data" collectively mean the total sum of necessary and sufficient conditions from which, once we know them all, we without further ado can deduce equilibrium price and quantity. In this second sense the distribution of wealth would thus, together with the other data, be a DETERMINANT though not the only determinant, of the prices and quantities of the various services and products bought and sold.

It will, however, be our main task in the paper to show that the distribution of wealth is not a "datum" in this second sense. Far from being an "independent variable" of the market process, it is, on the contrary, continuously subject to modification by the market forces. Needless to say, this is not to deny that at any moment it is among the forces that shape the path of the market process in the immediate future, but *it is* to deny that the mode of distribution as such can have any permanent influence. Though wealth is always distributed in some definite way, the mode of this distribution is ever-changing.

Only if the mode of distribution remained the same in period after period, while individual pieces of wealth were being transferred by inheritance, could such a constant mode be said to be a permanent economic force. In reality this is not so. The distribution of wealth is being shaped by the forces of the market as an object, not an agent, and whatever its mode may be today will soon have become an irrelevant bygone.

The distribution of wealth, therefore, has no place among the data of equilibrium. What is, however, of great economic and social interest is not the mode of distribution of wealth at a moment of time, but its mode of change over time. Such change, we shall see, finds its true place among the events that happen on that problematical "path" which may, but rarely in reality does, lead to equilibrium. It is a typically "dynamic" phenomenon. It is a curious fact that at a time when so much is heard of the need for the pursuit and promotion of dynamic studies it should arouse so little interest.

Ownership is a legal concept that refers to concrete material objects. Wealth is an economic concept that refers to scarce resources. All valuable resources are, or reflect, or embody, material objects, but not all material objects are resources: derelict houses and heaps of scrap are obvious examples, as are any objects that their owners would gladly give away if they could find somebody willing to remove them. Moreover, what is a resource today may cease to be one tomorrow, while what is a valueless object today may become valuable tomorrow. The resource status of material objects is therefore always problematical and depends to some extent on foresight. An object constitutes wealth only if it is a source of an income stream. The value of the object to the owner, actual or potential, reflects at any moment its expected income-yielding capacity. This, in its turn, will depend on the uses to which the object can be turned. The mere ownership of objects, therefore, does not necessarily confer wealth; it is their successful use that confers it. Not ownership but use of resources is the source of income and wealth. An ice-cream factory in New York may mean wealth to its owner; the same ice-cream factory in Greenland would scarcely be a resource.

In a world of unexpected change, the maintenance of wealth is always problematical; and in the long run it may be said to be impossible. In order to be able to maintain a given amount of wealth, which could be transferred by inheritance from one generation to the next, a family would have to own such resources as will yield a permanent net income stream, i.e., a stream of surplus of output value over the cost of factor services complementary to the resources owned. It seems that this would be possible only *either* in a stationary world, a world in which today is as yesterday and tomorrow like today, and in which thus, day after day, and year after year, the same income will accrue to the same owners or their heirs; *or* if all resource owners had perfect foresight. Since both cases are remote from reality we can safely ignore them. What, then, in reality happens to wealth in a world of unexpected change?

All wealth consists of capital assets that, in one way or another, embody or at least ultimately reflect the material resources of production, the sources of valuable output. All output is produced by human labor with the help of combinations of such resources. For this purpose, resources have to be used in certain combinations; complementarity is of the essence of resource use. The modes of this complementarity are in no way "given" to the entrepreneurs who make, initiate, and carry out production plans. There is in reality no such thing as *a* production function. On the contrary, the task of the entrepreneur consists precisely in finding, in a world of perpetual change, which combination of resources will yield, in the conditions of today, a maximum surplus of output over input value, and in guessing which will do so in the probable conditions of tomorrow, when output values, cost of complementary input, and technology all will have changed.

If all capital resources were infinitely versatile, the entrepreneurial problem would consist in no more than following the changes of external conditions by turning combinations of resources to a succession of uses made profitable by these changes. As it is, resources have, as a rule, a limited range of versatility; each is specific to a number of uses.[41] Hence, the need for adjustment to change will often entail the need for a change in the composition of the resource group, for "capital regrouping." But each change in the mode of complementarity will affect the value of the component resources by giving rise to capital gains and losses. Entrepreneurs will make higher bids for the services of those resources for which they have found more profitable uses, and lower bids for those which have to be turned to less profitable uses. In the limiting case where no (present or potential future) use can be found for a resource that has so far formed part of a profitable combination, this resource will lose its resource character altogether. But even in less drastic cases, capital gains and losses made on durable assets are an inevitable concomitant of a world of unexpected change.

The market process is thus seen to be a leveling process. In a market economy a process of redistribution of wealth is taking place all the time before which those outwardly similar processes that modern politicians are in the habit of instituting, pale into comparative insignificance, if for no other reason than that the market gives wealth to those who can hold it, while politicians give it to their constituents who, as a rule, cannot.

This process of redistribution of wealth is not prompted by a concatenation of hazards. Those who participate in it are not playing a game of chance, but a game of skill. This process, like all real dynamic processes, reflects the transmission of knowledge from mind to mind. It is possible only because some people have knowledge that others have not yet acquired, because knowledge of change and its implications spread gradually and unevenly throughout society.

In this process he is successful who understands earlier than anyone else that a certain resource, which today can be produced when it is new, or bought, when it is an existing resource, at a certain price A, will tomorrow form part of a productive combination as a result of which it will be worth A'. Such capital gains or losses prompted by the chance of, or need for, turning resources from one use to another, superior or inferior to the first, form the economic substance of what wealth means in a changing world, and are the chief vehicle of the process of redistribution.

In this process it is most unlikely that the same man will continue to be right in his guesses about possible new uses for existing or potential resources time after time, unless he is really superior. And in the latter case his heirs are unlikely to show similar success—unless they are superior, too. In a world of unexpected change, capital losses are ultimately as inevitable as are capital gains. Competition between capital owners and the specific nature of durable resources, even though it be "multiple specificity," entail that gains are followed by losses as losses are followed by gains.

These economic facts have certain social consequences. As the critics of the market economy nowadays prefer to take their stand on "social" grounds, it may be not inappropriate here to elucidate the true social results of the market process. We have already spoken of it as a leveling process. More aptly, we may now describe these results as an instance of what Pareto called "the circulation of elites." Wealth is unlikely to stay for long in the same hands. It passes from hand to hand as unforeseen change confers value, now on this, now on that specific resource, engendering capital gains and losses. The owners of wealth, we might say with Schumpeter, are like the guests at a hotel or the passengers in a train: they are always there but are never for long the same people.

In a market economy, we have seen, all wealth is of a problematical nature. The more durable assets are and the more specific, the more restricted the range of uses to which they may be turned, the more clearly the problem becomes visible. But in a society with little fixed capital in which most accumulated wealth took the form of stocks of commodities, mainly agricultural and perishable, carried for periods of various lengths, a society in which durable consumer goods, except perhaps for houses and furniture, hardly existed, the problem was not so clearly visible. Such was, by and large, the society in which the classical economists were living and from which they naturally borrowed many traits. In the conditions of their time, therefore, the classical economists were justified, up to a point, in regarding all capital as virtually homogeneous and perfectly versatile, contrasting it with land, the only specific and irreproducible resource. But in our time there is little or no justification for such a dichotomy. The more fixed capital there is, and the more durable it is, the greater the probability that such capital resources will, before they wear out, have to be used for purposes other than those for which they were originally designed. This means practically that in a modern market economy there can be no such thing as a source of permanent income. Durability and limited versatility make it impossible.

The main fact we have stressed in this paper, the redistribution of wealth caused by the forces of the market in a world of unexpected change, is a fact of common observation. Why, then, is it constantly being ignored? We could understand why the politicians choose to ignore it: after all, the large majority of their constituents are unlikely to be directly affected by it, and, as is amply shown in the case of inflation, would scarcely be able to understand it if they were. But why should economists choose to ignore it? That the mode of the distribution of wealth is a result of the operation of economic forces is the kind of proposition that, one would think, would appeal to them. Why, then, do so many economists continue to regard the distribution of wealth as a "datum" in the second sense mentioned above? We submit that the reason has to be sought in an excessive preoccupation with equilibrium problems.

We saw before that the successive modes of the distribution of wealth belong to the world of disequilibrium. Capital gains and losses arise in the main because durable resources have to be used in ways for which they were not planned, and because some men understand better and earlier than other men what the changing needs and resources of a world in motion imply. Equilibrium means consistency of plans, but the redistribution of wealth by the market is typically a result of inconsistent action. To those trained to think in equilibrium terms it is perhaps only natural that such processes as we have described should appear to be not quite "respectable." For them the "real" economic forces are those that tend to establish and maintain equilibrium. Forces only operating in disequilibrium are thus regarded as not really very interesting and are therefore all too often ignored.

We are not saying, of course, that the modern economist, so learned in the grammar of equilibrium, so ignorant of the facts of the market, is unable or unready to cope with economic change; that would be absurd. We are saying that he is well-equipped only to deal with types of change that happen to conform to a fairly rigid pattern.

Political and Economic Freedoms Together Spawn Humanity's Miracles

By Temba A. Nolutshungu

In this essay, the South African economist Temba A. Nolutshungu draws from his country's recent history to distinguish majority rule (which was won after decades of struggle against minority monopolization of power) from freedom, and shows the liberating potential of economic freedom.

Temba A. Nolutshungu is a director of the Free Market Foundation in South Africa. He teaches at economic empowerment programs throughout the country and is a frequent contributor to the South African press. He was a commissioner of the Zimbabwe Papers, a set of policy proposals for Zimbabwean recovery after the disaster of Mugabe's policies and submitted to Zimbabwean Prime Minister Morgan Tsvangirai. Nolutshungu was prominent during his youth in South Africa's Black Consciousness Movement.

In July 1794, Maximilien Robespierre, revolutionary republican, radical democrat and driving force behind the Reign of Terror in revolutionary France, during which some 40,000 French men and women died on the guillotine as "enemies of the nation," was put to death by his political opponents. Moments before his death, he addressed the mob that used to adulate him but now was baying for his blood, with the following words: "I gave you freedom; now you want bread as well." And with that ended the Reign of Terror.

The moral we can draw from this is that while there may be a link between political freedom and economic well-being, they are not the same thing.

Economic well-being is a consequence of freedom. In South Africa, with a formally recorded unemployment rate of 25.2 percent (a figure which does not include those who have given up looking for work), the disjuncture between political freedom and economic well-being reflects a potentially cataclysmic state of affairs—a danger exacerbated by successive political administrations repeatedly promising all sorts of benefits to their constituencies.

To deal with the challenges that face us, we have to clear away certain misconceptions.

Job creation is not a role of the state. For jobs to be sustainable, they have to be created by the private sector. Government-generated jobs are at the taxpayers' expense and amount to subsidized employment. Being unsustainable, they have no positive economic consequence. The private sector is the main creator of wealth, and the state sector a consumer.

Money is merely a medium of exchange for goods and services and should therefore relate to and reflect productivity. When I visited post-communist Russia and Czechoslovakia in 1991, the joke doing the rounds was that the workers pretended to work and the government pretended to pay them. Thus, in my opinion, when we talk about meaningful job creation we should focus solely on the private sector.

This begs the question as to which policies should apply to private enterprises. Which ones will enhance their productivity and which retard it? What should be done?

Let's examine the principles that underlie the simplest of exchanges between two parties. Simple transactions can serve as an example and a microcosm of the bigger economy. They should inform policymakers as to which policies are most compatible with human nature, because the human factor is pivotal in the economic context. Start far back in time with a hypothetical caveman who is skilled at hunting but inexpert at making a weapon for hunting. Our caveman meets a skilled weapon maker and agrees to exchange part of his quarry for a weapon. Both men come away from the transaction feeling they have profited by getting in return something of greater value to them than what they gave away. Sooner or later, the weapon maker finds that if he specializes in weapon making, instead of going hunting, he can barter the weapons for fur, meat, ivory and so on. He is in business. He prospers and all his customers prosper because they are now using more efficient hunting weapons.

What is important to note about this scenario is that there

is no force or fraud involved. No third-party involvement. No party that prescribes the rules of conducting business. The rules that the transacting parties uphold come about spontaneously. They comply as though with a natural order. This is what the late economist Friedrich Hayek referred to as the spontaneous order, and part of this order is that private property is reciprocally respected.

From this simple example, one can extrapolate that in the modern day economy, in a country where the government refrains from interfering in the economic arena, there will be high economic growth and concomitant socio-economic benefits. In other words, if a government promotes the economic freedom of producers and consumers and allows them to engage in transactions that do not entail force or fraud, the country, and its people, will prosper. This is a sure way to reduce unemployment, improve education, and create better health care.

These fundamental principles apply to all economies, regardless of the cultural context within which each has taken shape. The persistent "work ethic" myth warrants critical attention. This view implicitly reinforces national or ethnic group stereotypes in terms of having or lacking a work ethic, the logical extension of which is that the poor are poor because they lack a work ethic and the rich are more successful because they do have one—a very dangerous view to uphold, especially when it coincides with race.

Before the Berlin Wall came crashing down in 1989, West Germany was the second biggest economy in the world while East Germany was an economic disaster zone. These were the same people, same culture, and the same families in some cases before they were divided after World War II. A similar judgment can be made with regard to the two Koreas: the South an economic giant and the North an economic abyss that continues to absorb foreign aid. Again, same people, same culture. And what of the contrast between Mainland China and Hong Kong, before 1992 when Deng Xiaoping ushered in radical free market reforms after announcing that it was glorious to be rich and that it didn't matter if the cat was black or white so long as it caught mice? Yet again, same people, same culture, and the same telltale economic discrepancies. The difference was caused, every time, by the degree of freedom allowed to the economic actors.

Since 1992, thanks to the most radical free market reforms seen in recent years, China now looms large as the third biggest economy in the world. And sadly, in contrast, in the words of Bertel Schmitt, "the United States picked up that socialist economic playbook that Deng Xiaoping was smart enough to throw away."

The legislative and institutional framework within which economic activity takes place, and, in particular, the degree of regulation to which an economy is subjected, is the determinant of how wealthy a country and its inhabitants can be. In other words the degree to which governments allow individuals to exercise economic freedom will determine their economic outcome.

These words in 1986 by Professor Walter Williams, author of the thought-provoking book *South Africa's War Against Capitalism*, sum it all up: " . . . the solution to South Africa's problems is not special programs, it's not affirmative action, it's not handouts, and it's not welfare. It is freedom. Because if you look around the world and you look for rich people, diverse people who have the ability to get along fairly well, you are also looking at a society where there are relatively large amounts of individual freedom."

Section IV

Globalizing Capitalism

Global Capitalism and Justice

By June Arunga

In this essay, June Arunga calls for free-market capitalism in Africa and confronts those who oppose allowing Africans to engage in the world economy through freedom of trade. Her view is systematically supportive of free trade, as she criticizes those who support designated "trade zones" that offer special privileges (and sometimes violations of the property rights of local people) to foreign investors or privileged local elites and deny others freedom to trade or invest on an equal basis. She calls for respect for the property rights of African people and for free-market capitalism undistorted by privileges and monopoly powers.

June Arunga is a businesswoman and film producer from Kenya. She is the founder and CEO of Open Quest Media LLC and has worked with several telecom ventures in Africa. She made two BBC documentaries about Africa, The Devil's Footpath, *which documents her six-week, 5,000-mile trek from Cairo to Cape Town, and* Who's to Blame?, *which features a debate/dialogue between Arunga and former Ghanaian president Jerry Rawlings. She writes for AfricanLiberty.org and co-authored* The Cell Phone Revolution in Kenya. *Arunga received her law degree from the University of Buckingham in the United Kingdom.*

My experience is that the great bulk—maybe 90 percent—of disagreements stem from lack of information on one side or the other. That's especially important when people move from one cultural space to another. We are seeing a great surge of trade in Africa, among Africans, after a long period of isolation from each other due to protectionism, nationalism, and misunderstanding. I think we should celebrate that growth of trade. Some fear the increase of trade; I think that they need more information.

Globalization is happening and I think we should welcome it. It has created transfers of skills, access to technology from around the world, and much more. However, many have been kept out.

The question is why? I met the Swedish economist Johan Norberg, author of the eye-opening book *In Defense of Global Capitalism*, in 2002, and I was struck by how he dealt with information. He did not simply dismiss the opponents of free trade. Rather, he listened to them, considered their viewpoints, and verified their information. His interest in factual information is what initially led him to embrace capitalism.

I was also struck by how he took the perspective of the people most affected: the poor. Norberg has traveled the world asking questions. He doesn't tell people what they ought to think. He asks them what they think. By asking the poor who have been given opportunities to engage in trade—either as traders or merchants or as employees of enterprises involved in international trade—he revealed the facts that the official pontificators missed. Did that job at a new factory make your life better or worse? Did your first cell phone make your life better or worse? Has your income gone up or down? How do you travel: by foot, by bicycle, by motorbike, by car? Do you prefer to ride a motorbike or to walk? Norberg insists on looking at the facts on the ground. He asks the people involved what they think and whether free trade has improved their lives. He wants to hear individual perspectives.

We should ask what our governments are doing to us, not just for us. Our own governments are hurting us: they steal from us, they stop us from trading, and they keep the poor down. Local investors are not allowed to compete because of the lack of the rule of law in low-income countries. Maybe that's why they're low-income countries—because the people are not respected by their own governments.

Many governments of poor countries are focused on attracting "foreign investors," but they don't let their own people into the market. Opening up the market and competition to local people is not on their agendas. Local people have the insight, the understanding, and the "local knowledge." But our own governments in Africa keep their own people out of the market in favor of foreign or local special interest groups.

For example, heavy restrictions that stifle local competition in services, such as banking and water provision, ignore the abilities of our own people to use their local knowledge of technology, preferences, and infrastructure. It's not true "globalization" to give special favors to "foreign investors" when the locals are swept away and not allowed to compete. If the "special economic zones" that governments set up to attract "foreign investors" are a good idea, why can't the bulk of our people benefit from them? Why are they considered special zones of privilege, rather than a part of the freedom of trade for everyone? Freedom of trade should be about free competition to serve the people, not special privileges for local elites who don't want competition, or foreign investors who get special audiences with ministers.

It's not "free trade" when international companies can get special favors from governments and it's not "free trade" when local firms are blocked by their own government from the market. Free trade requires the rule of law for all and freedom for all to engage in the most natural of actions: voluntary exchange.

Our prosperity as Africans won't come from foreign aid or easy money. We've had plenty of that in Africa, but it hasn't had a positive impact on the lives of the poor. That kind of "aid" spawns corruption and undermines the rule of law. It comes tied to purchasing services from specific people in the countries that are sending the aid. That's distortive of trade relations. But worst of all, "aid" disconnects governments from their own people, because the people who are paying the bills are not in Africa, but in Paris, Washington, or Brussels.

Trade can be distorted and made unfree by local elites who get the minister's ear through, well, you know how. Trade can be distorted by granting monopoly rights to the exclusion of both local and foreign competitors. Furthermore, trade is distorted and made unfree when foreign elites get monopoly rights from local governments through tied-aid deals in collusion with their own governments: deals that exclude both local and foreign competitors since the deal is fixed. All of these regulations restrict our markets and our freedom. We are left purchasing goods and services that may not be of the highest quality or the best price, because we don't have freedom of choice. That lack of freedom keeps us down and perpetuates poverty.

We aren't just robbed of lower prices and better quality, though. We are robbed of the opportunity to innovate, to make use of our minds, to improve our situations through our own energy and intellect. In the long run, that is the greater crime against us. Protectionism and privilege perpetuate not only economic bankruptcy, but stagnation of intellect, courage, character, will, determination, and faith in ourselves.

What we need is information. We need to talk to people on the ground. We need to check the same facts. In most cases, they're not secrets, but few even bother to look. The evidence is overwhelming that free-market capitalism, freedom of trade, and equal rights under the rule of law create prosperity for the masses of people.

What we need is free-market capitalism that creates the space for us to realize our potential. The Peruvian economist Hernando de Soto, in his book *The Mystery of Capital*, shows how poor people can convert "dead capital" into "living capital" to improve their lives. Lack of capital is not inevitable. We in Africa have so much capital, but most of it cannot be put to use to improve our lives. It's "dead." We need to improve our property rights to make our abundant capital the "living capital" that generates life. We need property, that is, we need our rights to be respected. We need equality before the law. We need free-market capitalism.

Human Betterment through Globalization

By Vernon Smith

In this essay, economist and Nobel Laureate Vernon Smith traces the growth of human wealth through the spread of markets and explains why global capitalism generates human betterment.

Vernon Smith is professor of economics at Chapman University in California and a pioneer in the emerging field of "experimental economics." His research has focused on commodity and capital markets, the emergence of asset bubbles, business cycles, finance, natural resource economics, and the growth of market institutions. In 2002 he shared the Nobel Prize in Economics for "having established laboratory experiments as a tool in empirical economic analysis, especially in the study of alternative market mechanisms." *He has published widely in academic journals of economics, game theory, and risk, and is the author of* Papers in Experimental Economics *and* Bargaining and Market Behavior: Essays in Experimental Economics. *Smith is also world renowned as a teacher and has developed programs to utilize experimental economics not only to generate new insights into economic processes, but also to teach the principles of economics.*

This essay is excerpted from a speech delivered at "Evenings at FEE" in September 2005.

My message today is an optimistic one. It is about exchange and markets, which allow us to engage in task and knowledge specialization. It is this specialization that is the secret of all wealth creation and the only source of sustainable human betterment. This is the essence of globalization.

The challenge is that we all function simultaneously in two overlapping worlds of exchange. First, we live in a world of personal, social exchange based on reciprocity and shared norms in small groups, families, and communities. The phrase "I owe you one" is a human universal across many languages in which people voluntarily acknowledge indebtedness for a favor. From primitive times, personal exchange allowed specialization of tasks (hunting, gathering, and tool making) and laid the basis for enhanced productivity and welfare. This division of labor made it possible for early men to migrate all over the world. Thus, specialization started globalization long before the emergence of formal markets.

Second, we live in a world of impersonal market exchange where communication and cooperation gradually developed through long-distance trade between strangers. In acts of personal exchange we usually intend to do good for others. In the marketplace this perception is often lost as each of us tends to focus on our own personal gain. However, our controlled laboratory experiments demonstrate that the same individuals who go out of their way to cooperate in personal exchange strive to maximize their own gain in a larger market. Without intending to do so, in their market transactions they also maximize the joint benefit received by the group. Why? Because of property rights. In personal exchange the governing rules emerge by voluntary consent of the parties. In impersonal market exchange, the governing rules—such as property rights, which prohibit taking without giving in return—are encoded in the institutional framework. Hence the two worlds of exchange function in a similar way: you have to give in order to receive.

The Foundation of Prosperity

Commodity and service markets, which are the foundation of wealth creation, determine the extent of specialization. In organized markets, producers experience relatively predictable costs of production, and consumers rely on a relatively predictable supply of valued goods. These constantly repeated market activities are incredibly efficient, even in very complex market relationships with multiple commodities being traded.

We have also discovered through our market experiments that people generally deny that any kind of model can predict their final trading prices and the volume of goods they will buy and sell. In fact, market efficiency does not require a large number of participants, complete information, economic understanding, or any particular sophistication. After all, people were trading in markets long before there existed any economists to study the market process. All you have to know is when you are making more money or less money and whether you have a chance to modify your actions.

The hallmark of commodity and service markets is diversity—a diversity of tastes, human skills, knowledge, natural resources, soil, and climate. But diversity without freedom to exchange implies poverty. No human being, even if abundantly endowed with a single skill or a single resource, can prosper without trade. Through free markets we depend on others whom we do not know, recognize, or even understand. Without markets we would indeed be poor, miserable, brutish, and ignorant.

Markets require consensual enforcement of the rules of social interaction and economic exchange. No one has said it better than David Hume over 250 years ago—there are just three laws of nature: the right of possession, transference by consent, and the performance of promises. These are the ultimate foundations of order that make possible markets and prosperity.

Hume's laws of nature derive from the ancient commandments: thou shalt not steal, thou shalt not covet thy neighbor's possessions, and thou shalt not bear false witness. The "stealing" game consumes wealth and discourages its reproduction. Coveting the property of others invites a coercive state to redistribute wealth, thus endangering incentives to produce tomorrow's harvest. Bearing false witness undermines community, management credibility, investor trust, long-term profitability, and the personal exchanges that are most humanizing.

Only Markets Deliver the Goods

Economic development is linked with free economic and political systems nurtured by the rule of law and private property rights. Strong centrally planned regimes, wherever attempted, have failed to deliver the goods. There are, however, plenty of examples of both big and small countries (from China to New Zealand and Ireland) where governments have removed at least some barriers to economic freedom. These countries have witnessed remarkable economic growth by simply letting people pursue their own economic betterment.

China has moved considerably in the direction of economic freedom. Just over a year ago China revised its constitution to allow people to own, buy, and sell private property. Why? One of the problems the Chinese government encountered was that people were buying and selling property even though those transactions were not recognized by the government. This invited local officials to collect from those who were breaking the law by trading. By recognizing property rights, the central government is trying to undercut the source of power that supports local bureaucratic corruption, which is very hard to centrally monitor and control. This constitutional change, as I see it, is a practical means to limit rampant government corruption and political interference with economic development.

Though this change has not resulted from any political predisposition for liberty, it may very well pave the way toward a freer society. The immediate benefits are already there: 276 of the Fortune 500 companies are currently investing in a huge R&D park near Beijing, based on very favorable 50-year lease terms from the Chinese government.

The case of Ireland illustrates the principle that you don't have to be a big country to grow wealthy through liberalizing government economic policy. In the past, Ireland was a major exporter of people. This worked to the advantage of the United States and Great Britain, who received many bright Irish immigrants fleeing the stultifying life of their homeland. Only two decades ago Ireland was mired in third-world poverty, but has now surpassed its former colonial master in income per capita, becoming a committed European player. According to World Bank statistics, Ireland's growth rate of Gross Domestic Product (GDP) jumped from 3.2 percent in the 1980s to 7.8 percent in the 1990s. Ireland recently was the eighth highest in GDP per capita in the world, while the United Kingdom was fifteenth. By fostering direct foreign investment (including venture capital) and promoting financial services and information technology, Ireland has experienced a formidable brain-drain reversal—young people are coming back home.

These young people are returning because of new opportunities made possible by expansion of economic freedom in their homeland. They are examples of "can-do" knowledge-based entrepreneurs who are creating wealth and human betterment not only for their native country, but also for the United States and all other countries around the world. These people's stories demonstrate how bad government policies can be changed to create new economic opportunities that can dramatically reverse a country's brain drain.

We Have Nothing to Fear

An essential part of the process of change, growth, and economic betterment is to allow yesterday's jobs to follow the path of yesterday's technology. Preventing domestic companies from outsourcing will not stop their foreign competitors from doing so. Through outsourcing, foreign competitors will be able to lower their costs, use the savings to lower prices and upgrade technology, and thus gain a big advantage in the market.

One of the best-known examples of outsourcing was the New England textile industry's move to the South after World War II in response to lower wages in the Southern states. (As was to be expected, this raised wages in the South, and the industry eventually had to move on to lower-cost sources in Asia.)

But the jobs did not vanish in New England. The textile business was replaced by high-tech industries: electronic information and biotechnology. This resulted in huge net gains to New England even though it lost what had once been an important industry. In 1965 Warren Buffett gained control of Berkshire-Hathaway, one of those fading textile makers in Massachusetts. He used the company's large but declining cash flow as a launch pad for reinvesting the money in a host of undervalued business ventures. They became famously successful, and 40 years later Buffett's company has a market capitalization of $113 billion. The same transition is occurring today with K-Mart and Sears Roebuck. Nothing is forever: as old businesses decline, their resources are diverted to new ones.

The National Bureau of Economic Research has just reported

a new study of domestic and foreign investment by U.S. multinational corporations. The study demonstrated that for every dollar invested in a foreign country, they invest three and a half dollars in the United States. This proves that there is a complementary relationship between foreign and domestic investment: when one increases, the other increases as well. McKinsey and Company estimates that for every dollar U.S. companies outsource to India, $1.14 accrues to the benefit of the United States. About half of this benefit is returned to investors and customers and most of the remainder is spent on new jobs that have been created. By contrast, in Germany every Euro invested abroad only generates an 80 percent benefit to the domestic economy, mainly because the reemployment rate of displaced German workers is so much lower due to the vast number of government regulations.

I believe that as long as the United States remains number one on the world innovation index, we have nothing to fear from outsourcing and much to fear if our politicians succeed in opposing it. According to the Institute for International Economics, more than one hundred and fifteen thousand higher-paying computer software jobs were created in 1999–2003, while seventy thousand jobs were eliminated due to outsourcing. Similarly in the service sector twelve million new jobs were being created while ten million old jobs were being replaced. This phenomenon of rapid technological change and the replacement of old jobs with new ones is what economic development is all about.

By outsourcing to foreign countries, American businesses save money that enables them to invest in new technologies and new jobs in order to remain competitive in the world market. Unfortunately, we cannot enjoy the benefits without incurring the pain of transition. Change is certainly painful. It is painful for those who lose their jobs and must seek new careers. It is painful for those who risk investment in new technologies and lose. But the benefits captured by winners generate great new wealth for the economy as a whole. These benefits, in turn, are consolidated across the market through the discovery process and competitive learning experience.

Globalization is not new. It is a modern word describing an ancient human movement, a word for mankind's search for betterment through exchange and the worldwide expansion of specialization. It is a peaceful word. In the wise pronouncement of the great French economist Frederic Bastiat, if goods don't cross borders, soldiers will.

The Culture of Liberty

By Mario Vargas Llosa

In this essay, the novelist and Nobel Laureate in Literature Mario Vargas Llosa dispels fears of global capitalism contaminating or eroding cultures and argues that notions of "collective identity" are dehumanizing and that identity springs from the "capacity of human beings to resist these influences and counter them with free acts of their own invention."

Mario Vargas Llosa is a world-renowned novelist and public intellectual. In 2010 he was awarded the Nobel Prize in Literature "for his cartography of structures of power and his trenchant images of the individual's resistance, revolt, and defeat." He is the author of such works of fiction as The Feast of the Goat, The War of the End of the World, Aunt Julia and the Scriptwriter, The Bad Girl, The Real Life of Alejandro Mayta, *and many others.*

This essay is reprinted by permission of the author from the January 1, 2001, issue of Foreign Policy.

The most effective attacks against globalization are usually not those related to economics. Instead, they are social, ethical, and, above all, cultural. These arguments surfaced amid the tumult of Seattle in 1999 and have resonated more recently in Davos, Bangkok, and Prague. They say this:

> The disappearance of national borders and the establishment of a world interconnected by markets will deal a deathblow to regional and national cultures and to the traditions, customs, myths, and mores that determine each country or region's cultural identity. Since most of the world is incapable of resisting the invasion of cultural products from developed countries—or, more to the point, from the superpower, the United States—that inevitably trails the great transnational corporations, North American culture will ultimately impose itself, standardizing the world and annihilating its rich flora

of diverse cultures. In this manner, all other peoples, and not just the small and weak ones, will lose their identity, their soul, and will become no more than twenty-first-century colonies—zombies or caricatures modeled after the cultural norms of a new imperialism that, in addition to ruling over the planet with its capital, military might, and scientific knowledge, will impose on others its language and its ways of thinking, believing, enjoying, and dreaming.

This nightmare or negative utopia of a world that, thanks to globalization, is losing its linguistic and cultural diversity and is being culturally appropriated by the United States, is not the exclusive domain of left-wing politicians nostalgic for Marx, Mao, or Che Guevara. This delirium of persecution—spurred by hatred and rancor toward the North American giant—is also apparent in developed countries and nations of high culture and is shared among political sectors of the left, center, and right.

The most notorious case is that of France, where we see frequent government campaigns in defense of a French "cultural identity" supposedly threatened by globalization. A vast array of intellectuals and politicians is alarmed by the possibility that the soil that produced Montaigne, Descartes, Racine, and Baudelaire—and a country that was long the arbiter of fashion in clothing, thought, art, dining, and in all domains of the spirit— can be invaded by McDonald's, Pizza Hut, Kentucky Fried Chicken, rock, rap, Hollywood movies, blue jeans, sneakers, and T-shirts. This fear has resulted, for instance, in massive French subsidies for the local film industry and demands for quotas requiring theaters to show a certain number of national films and limit the importation of movies from the United States. This fear is also the reason why municipalities issued severe directives penalizing with high fines any publicity announcements that littered with Anglicisms the language of Molière. (Although, judging by the view of a pedestrian on the streets of Paris, the directives were not quite respected.) This is the reason why José Bové, the farmer-cum-crusader against *la malbouffe* (lousy food), has become no less than a popular hero in France. And with his recent sentencing to three months in prison, his popularity has likely increased.

Even though I believe this cultural argument against globalization is unacceptable, we should recognize that deep within it lies an unquestionable truth. This century, the world in which we will live will be less picturesque and imbued with less local color than the one we left behind. The festivals, attire, customs, ceremonies, rites, and beliefs that in the past gave humanity its folkloric and ethnological variety are progressively disappearing or confining themselves to minority sectors, while the bulk of society abandons them and adopts others more suited to the reality of our time. All countries of the earth experience this process, some more quickly than others, but it is not due to globalization. Rather, it is due to modernization, of which the former is effect, not cause. It is possible to lament, certainly, that this process occurs, and to feel nostalgia for the eclipse of the past ways of life that, particularly from our comfortable vantage point of the present, seem full of amusement, originality, and color. But this process is unavoidable. Totalitarian regimes in countries like Cuba or North Korea, fearful that any opening will destroy them, close themselves off and issue all types of prohibitions and censures against modernity. But even they are unable to impede modernity's slow infiltration and its gradual undermining of their so-called cultural identity. In theory, perhaps, a country could keep this identity, but only if—like certain remote tribes in Africa or the Amazon—it decides to live in total isolation, cutting off all exchange with other nations and practicing self-sufficiency. A cultural identity preserved in this form would take that society back to prehistoric standards of living.

It is true that modernization makes many forms of traditional life disappear. But at the same time, it opens opportunities and constitutes an important step forward for a society as a whole. That is why, when given the option to choose freely, peoples, sometimes counter to what their leaders or intellectual traditionalists would like, opt for modernization without the slightest ambiguity.

The allegations against globalization and in favor of cultural identity reveal a static conception of culture that has no historical basis. Which cultures have ever remained identical and unchanged over time? To find them we must search among the small and primitive magical-religious communities that live in caves, worship thunder and beasts, and, due to their primitivism, are increasingly vulnerable to exploitation and extermination. All other cultures, in particular those that have the right to be called modern and alive, have evolved to the point that they are but a remote reflection of what they were just two or three generations before. This evolution is easily apparent in countries like France, Spain, and England, where the changes over the last half century have been so spectacular and profound that a Marcel Proust, a Federico García Lorca, or a Virginia Woolf would hardly recognize today the societies in which they were born— the societies their works helped so much to renew.

The notion of "cultural identity" is dangerous. From a social point of view, it represents merely a doubtful, artificial concept, but from a political perspective it threatens humanity's most precious achievement: freedom. I do not deny that people who speak the same language, were born and live in the same territory, face the same problems, and practice the same religions and customs have common characteristics. But that collective denominator can never fully define each one of them, and it only abolishes or relegates to a disdainful secondary plane the sum of unique attributes and traits that differentiates one member of the group from the others. The concept of identity, when not employed on an exclusively individual scale, is inherently reductionist and dehumanizing, a collectivist and ideological abstraction of all that is original and creative in the human being, of all that has not been imposed by inheritance, geography, or social pressure. Rather, true identity springs from the capacity of human beings to resist these influences and counter them with free acts of their own invention.

The notion of "collective identity" is an ideological fiction and the foundation of nationalism. For many ethnologists and anthropologists, collective identity does not represent the truth even among the most archaic communities. Common practices and customs may be crucial to the defense of a group, but the margin of initiative and creativity among its members to emancipate themselves from the group is invariably large, and individual differences prevail over collective traits when individuals are examined on their own terms, and not as mere peripheral elements of collectivity. Globalization extends radically to all citizens of this planet the possibility to construct their individual cultural identities through voluntary action, according to their preferences and intimate motivations. Now, citizens are not always obligated, as in the past and in many places in the present, to respect an identity that traps them in a concentration camp from which there is no escape—the identity that is imposed on them through the language, nation, church, and customs of the place where they were born. In this sense, globalization must be welcomed because it notably expands the horizons of individual liberty.

One Continent's Two Histories

Perhaps Latin America is the best example of the artifice and absurdity of trying to establish collective identities. What might be Latin America's cultural identity? What would be included in a coherent collection of beliefs, customs, traditions, practices, and mythologies that endows this region with a singular personality, unique and nontransferable? Our history has been forged in intellectual polemics—some ferocious— seeking to answer this question. The most celebrated was the one that, beginning in the early twentieth century, pitted Hispanists against indigenists and reverberated across the continent.

For Hispanists like José de la Riva Agüero, Victor Andrés Belaúnde, and Francisco García Calderón—Latin America was born when, thanks to the Discovery and the Conquest, it joined with the Spanish and Portuguese languages and, adopting Christianity, came to form part of Western civilization. Hispanists did not belittle pre-Hispanic cultures, but considered that these constituted but a layer—and not the primary one—of the social and historical reality that only completed its nature and personality thanks to the vivifying influence of the West.

Indigenists, on the other hand, rejected with moral indignation the alleged benefits that Europeans brought to Latin America. For them, our identity finds its roots and its soul in pre-Hispanic cultures and civilizations, whose development and modernization were brutally stunted by violence and subjected to censure, repression, and marginalization not only during the three colonial centuries but also later, after the advent of republicanism. According to indigenist thinkers, the authentic "American expression" (to use the title of a book by José Lezama Lima) resides in all the cultural manifestations—from the native languages to the beliefs, rites, arts, and popular mores—that resisted Western cultural oppression and endured to our days. A distinguished historian of this vein, the Peruvian Luis E. Valcárcel, even affirmed that the churches, convents, and other monuments of colonial architecture should be burned since they represented the "Anti-Peru." They were impostors, a negation of the pristine American identity that could only be of exclusively indigenous roots. And one of Latin America's most original novelists, José María Arguedas, narrated, in stories of great delicacy and vibrant moral protest, the epic of the survival of the Quechua culture in the Andean world, despite the suffocating and distortionary presence of the West.

Hispanicism and indigenism produced excellent historical essays and highly creative works of fiction, but, judged from our current perspective, both doctrines seem equally sectarian, reductionist, and false. Neither is capable of fitting the expansive diversity of Latin America into its ideological straitjacket, and both smack of racism. Who would dare claim in our day that only what is "Hispanic" or "Indian" legitimately represents Latin America? Nevertheless, efforts to forge and isolate our distinct "cultural identity" continue today with a political and intellectual zeal deserving of worthier causes. Seeking to impose a cultural identity on a people is equivalent to locking them in a prison and denying them the most precious of liberties—that of choosing what, how, and who they want to be. Latin America has not one but many cultural identities; no one of them can claim more legitimacy or purity than the others.

Of course, Latin America embodies the pre-Hispanic world and its cultures, which, in Mexico, Guatemala, and the Andean countries, still exert so much social force. But Latin America is also a vast swarm of Spanish and Portuguese speakers with a tradition of five centuries behind them whose presence and actions have been decisive in giving the continent its current features. And is not Latin America also something of Africa, which arrived on our shores together with Europe? Has not the African presence indelibly marked our skin, our music, our idiosyncrasies, our society? The cultural, ethnic, and social ingredients that make up Latin America link us to almost all the regions and cultures of the world. We have so many cultural identities that it is like not having one at all. This reality is, contrary to what nationalists believe, our greatest treasure. It is also an excellent credential that enables us to feel like full-fledged citizens in our globalized world.

Local Voices, Global Reach

The fear of Americanization of the planet is more ideological paranoia than reality. There is no doubt, of course, that with globalization, English has become the general language of our time, as was Latin in the Middle Ages. And it will continue its ascent, since it is an indispensable instrument for international transactions and communication. But does this mean that English necessarily develops at the expense of the other great languages? Absolutely not. In fact, the opposite is true. The vanishing of borders and an increasingly interdependent world have created incentives for new generations to learn and assimilate to other cultures, not merely as a hobby but also out of necessity, since the ability to speak several languages and navigate comfortably in different cultures has become crucial for professional success. Consider the case of Spanish. Half a century ago, Spanish speakers were an inward-looking community; we projected ourselves in only very limited ways beyond our traditional linguistic confines. Today, Spanish is dynamic and thriving, gaining beachheads or even vast landholdings on all five continents. The fact that there are some twenty-five to thirty million Spanish speakers in the United States today explains why the two recent U.S. presidential candidates, Texas Governor George W. Bush and Vice President Al Gore, campaigned not only in English but also in Spanish.

How many millions of young men and women around the globe have responded to the challenges of globalization by learning Japanese, German, Mandarin, Cantonese, Russian, or French? Fortunately, this tendency will only increase in the coming years.

That is why the best defense of our own cultures and languages is to promote them vigorously throughout this new world, not to persist in the naïve pretense of vaccinating them against the menace of English. Those who propose such remedies speak much about culture, but they tend to be ignorant people who mask their true vocation: nationalism. And if there is anything at odds with the universalist propensities of culture, it is the parochial, exclusionary, and confused vision that nationalist perspectives try to impose on cultural life. The most admirable lesson that cultures teach us is that they need not be protected by bureaucrats or commissars, or confined behind iron bars, or isolated by customs services in order to remain alive and exuberant; to the contrary, such efforts would only wither or even trivialize culture. Cultures must live freely, constantly jousting with different cultures. This renovates and renews them, allowing them to evolve and adapt to the continuous flow of life. In antiquity, Latin did not kill Greek; to the contrary, the artistic originality and intellectual depth of Hellenic culture permeated Roman civilization and, through it, the poems of Homer and the philosophies of Plato and Aristotle reached the entire world. Globalization will not make local cultures disappear; in a framework of worldwide openness, all that is valuable and worthy of survival in local cultures will find fertile ground in which to bloom.

This is happening in Europe, everywhere. Especially noteworthy is Spain, where regional cultures are reemerging with special vigor. During the dictatorship of General Francisco Franco, regional cultures were repressed and condemned to a clandestine existence. But with the return of democracy, Spain's rich cultural diversity was unleashed and allowed to develop freely. In the country's regime of autonomies, local cultures have had an extraordinary boom, particularly in Catalonia, Galicia, and the Basque country, but also in the rest of Spain. Of course, we must not confuse this regional cultural rebirth, which is positive and enriching, with the phenomenon of nationalism, which poses serious threats to the culture of liberty.

In his celebrated 1948 essay "Notes Towards the Definition of Culture," T.S. Eliot predicted that in the future, humanity would experience a renaissance of local and regional cultures. At the time, his prophecy seemed quite daring. However, globalization will likely make it a reality in the twenty-first century, and we must be happy about this. A rebirth of small, local cultures will give back to humanity that rich multiplicity of behavior and expressions that the nation-state annihilated in order to create so-called national cultural identities toward the end of the eighteenth, and particularly in the nineteenth, century. (This fact is easily forgotten, or we attempt to forget it because of its grave moral connotations.) National cultures were often forged in blood and fire, prohibiting the teaching or publication of vernacular languages or the practice of religions and customs that dissented from those the nation-state considered ideal. In this way, in many countries of the world, the nation-state forcibly imposed a dominant culture upon local ones that were repressed and abolished from official life. But, contrary to the warnings of those who fear globalization, it is not easy to completely erase cultures—however small they may be—if behind them is a rich tradition and people who practice them, even if in secret. And today, thanks to the weakening of the nation-state, we are seeing forgotten, marginalized, and silenced local cultures reemerging and displaying dynamic signs of life in the great concert of this globalized planet.

A Little Further Reading for Fun and Profit (and Better School Papers)

The literature on the morality of capitalism is vast. Most of it is rubbish. Here are a few readable books that you should find helpful in understanding the issues surrounding capitalism. The list could be a lot longer, but many other books and essays are already cited in the essays in The Morality of Capitalism, *including the works of Smith, Mises, Hayek, Rand, McCloskey, and other defenders of free-market capitalism. So don't be afraid to track down endnoted items in the essays in this book. That said, the books listed below alphabetically by name of author or editor should provide some useful mental exercise.*

—*Tom G. Palmer*

The Morals of Markets and Related Essays, by H. B. Acton (Indianapolis: Liberty Fund, 1993). The British philosopher H. B. Acton wrote clearly and sensibly about profit, competition, individualism and collectivism, planning, and many other topics.

Morals and Markets: An Evolutionary Account of the Modern World, by Daniel Friedman (New York: Palgrave Macmillan, 2008). The author offers insights into the parallel evolution of markets and morality and makes some controversial suggestions for improving both.

The Fatal Conceit: The Errors of Socialism, by F. A. Hayek (Chicago: University of Chicago Press, 1988). Hayek received the Nobel Prize in economic science, but was no "mere economist." This short book—his last—draws together many of his research interests to present a sweeping case for free-market capitalism.

The Ethics of Redistribution, by Bertrand de Jouvenel (Indianapolis: Liberty Fund, 1990). This very short book is based on lectures given at Cambridge University by the famous French political scientist. The chapters are short and concise and examine the ethical foundations and implications of attempts to redistribute income to achieve greater income equality.

Discovery and the Capitalist Process, by Israel Kirzner (Chicago: University of Chicago Press, 1985). An "Austrian" economist examines capitalism, interventionism, and socialism through the lens of entrepreneurship, and has a lot of interesting things to say about alertness, innovation, incentives, and profits.

The Ethics of the Market, by John Meadowcraft (New York: Palgrave Macmillan, 2005). A very short overview of issues raised by a variety of enemies of free-market capitalism.

The Origins of Virtue: Human Instincts and the Evolution of Cooperation, by Matt Ridley (New York: Viking, 1997). Ridley is a zoologist and professional science writer who has applied his intellect to understanding human behavior through the lens of evolutionary biology. His insights into virtue, property, and trade are helpful and fun to read.

The Economics of Rights, Co-operation, and Welfare, by Robert Sugden (London: Palgrave Macmillan, 2005). The author offers a very accessible look at the morality of property and exchange through the lens of game theory. The mathematics is very basic (really) and helps us to understand the great insights of the philosopher David Hume.

Moral Markets: The Critical Role of Values in the Economy, ed. by Paul J. Zak (Princeton: Princeton University Press, 2008). The essays in this book explore many topics about the morality of markets and present advanced scientific insights from game theory, biology, psychology, and other disciplines.

Dr. Tom G. Palmer is executive vice president for international programs at the Atlas Network and oversees the work of teams working around the world to advance the principles of classical liberalism. Dr. Palmer is a senior fellow of the Cato Institute, where he was formerly vice president for international programs and director of the Center for the Promotion of Human Rights. Palmer was an H. B. Earhart Fellow at Hertford College, Oxford University, and a vice president of the Institute for Humane Studies at George Mason University. He is a member of the board of advisors of Students For Liberty. He has published reviews and articles on politics and morality in scholarly journals such as the *Harvard Journal of Law and Public Policy*, *Ethics*, *Critical Review*, and *Constitutional Political Economy*, as well as in publications such as *Slate*, the *Wall Street Journal*, the *New York Times*, *Die Welt*, *Al Hayat*, *Caixing*, the *Washington Post*, and *The Spectator* of London. He received his B.A. in liberal arts from St. Johns College in Annapolis, Maryland; his M.A. in philosophy from The Catholic University of America, Washington, D.C.; and his doctorate in politics from Oxford University. His scholarship has been published in books from Princeton University Press, Cambridge University Press, Routledge, and other academic publishers and he is the author of *Realizing Freedom: Libertarian Theory, History, and Practice*, published in 2009.

Notes

Introduction: The Morality of Capitalism

1 Robert Nozick, *Anarchy, State, and Utopia* (New York: Basic Books, 1974), p. 163.

2 Joyce Appleby, *The Relentless Revolution: A History of Capitalism* (New York: W. W. Norton and Co., 2010), pp. 25-26.

3 David Schwab and Elinor Ostrom, "The Vital Role of Norms and Rules in Maintaining Open Public and Private Economies," in *Moral Markets: The Critical Role of Values in the Economy*, ed. by Paul J. Zak (Princeton: Princeton University Press, 2008), pp. 204-27.

4 Deirdre McCloskey, *Bourgeois Dignity: Why Economics Can't Explain the Modern World* (Chicago: University of Chicago Press, 2010), p. 48.

5 For a simple arithmetic explanation of the principle of comparative advantage, see tomgpalmer.com/wpcontent/uploads/papers/The%20Economics%20of%20Comparative%20Advantage.doc.

6 For a remarkable account of the general decline of the experience of force in human affairs, see James L. Payne, *A History of Force* (Sandpoint, Idaho: Lytton Publishing, 2004).

7 Envy as an impulse harmful to social cooperation and inimical to free-market capitalism has been studied by many thinkers. A recent and interesting approach that draws on the Indian classic epic *The Mahabharata* can be found in Gurcharan Das, *The Difficulty of Being Good: On the Subtle Art of Dharma* (New York: Oxford University Press, 2009), esp. pp. 1-32.

8 Fernand Braudel, *Civilization and Capitalism, 15th–18th Century: The Wheels of Commerce* (New York: Harper & Row, 1982), p. 232.

9 Ibid., p. 236.

10 Louis Blanc, *Organisation du Travail* (Paris: Bureau de la Societé de l'Industrie Fraternelle, 1847), cited in Braudel, *Civilization and Capitalism, 15th–18th Century: The Wheels of Commerce*, op. cit., p. 237.

11 Karl Marx and Frederick Engels, *Manifesto of the Communist Party*, in Karl Marx and Frederick Engels, *Collected Works, Volume 6* (1976: Progress Publishers, Moscow), p. 489.

12 For a devastating seminal critique of Marx's economic theories, see Eugen von Böhm-Bawerk, *Karl Marx and the Close of His System* (1896; New York: Augustus M. Kelley, 1949). A better translation of Böhm-Bawerk's title would be, "On the Conclusion of the Marxian System." Böhm-Bawerk refers in his title to the publication of the third volume of Capital, which "concluded" the Marxian system. It should be noted that Böhm-Bawerk's criticism is altogether an internal critique, and does not rest in any way on the results of the "marginal revolution" in economic science that took place in 1870. See also the essay by Ludwig von Mises, "Economic Calculation in the Socialist Commonwealth," in F. A. Hayek, ed., *Collectivist Economic Planning* (London: George Routledge & Sons, 1935) on the inability of collectivism to solve the problem of economic calculation.

13 Karl Marx, "The Eighteenth Brumaire of Louis Bonaparte," in David Fernbach, ed., *Karl Marx: Surveys from Exile: Political Writings, Volume II* (New York: Vintage Books, 1974), p. 186. I describe the contradictions and confusions of Marxian economic and social analysis in "Classical Liberalism, Marxism, and the Conflict of Classes: The Classical Liberal Theory of Class Conflict," in *Realizing Freedom: Libertarian Theory, History, and Practice* (Washington: Cato Institute, 2009), pp. 255-75.

14   Karl Marx and Friedrich Engels, *Manifesto of the Communist Party*, p. 488.

15   Karl Marx, "The Eighteenth Brumaire of Louis Bonaparte," p. 222.

16   Karl Marx, "The Eighteenth Brumaire of Louis Bonaparte," p. 238.

17   Shirley M. Gruner, *Economic Materialism and Social Moralism* (The Hague: Mouton, 1973), pp. 189–190.

18   See, for example, Sheldon Richman, "Is Capitalism Something Good?" www.thefreemanonline.org/columns/tgif/is-capitalism-something-good/.

19   Joseph Schumpeter, *Capitalism, Socialism, and Democracy* (London: Routledge, 2006), p. 84.

20   David Boaz, "Creating a Framework for Utopia," *The Futurist*, December 24, 1996, www.cato.org/pub_display.php?pub_id=5976.

21   The legal historian Henry Sumner Maine famously described "the movement of the progressive societies" from inherited relations, based on family membership to personal liberty and civil society as "a movement from Status to Contract." Henry Sumner Maine, *Ancient Law* (Brunswick, NJ: Transaction Publishers, 2003), p. 170.

22   Leo Melamed, "Reminiscences of a Refugee," in *For Crying Out Loud: From Open Outcry to the Electronic Screen* (Hoboken, NJ: John Wiley & Sons, 2009), p. 136.

23   I address the issue of poverty and free-market capitalism more systematically in "Classical Liberalism, Poverty, and Morality," in *Poverty and Morality: Religious and Secular Perspectives*, William A. Galston and Peter H. Hoffenberg, eds. (New York: Cambridge University Press, 2010), pp. 83-114.

24   This is an especially common attitude among philosophers, perhaps the saddest of whom was the late G. A. Cohen, who devoted much of his intellectual career to attempting, but failing, to refute Nozick's one thought experiment. Citations to Cohen's articles and a demonstration of the failure of his critique can be found in "G. A. Cohen on Self-Ownership, Property, and Equality," in *Realizing Freedom*, pp. 139-54.

25   Quoted in Michael Sandel, *Justice: What's the Right Thing to Do?* (New York: Farrar, Straus, and Giroux, 2009), p. 61.

26   Milton Friedman, Capitalism and Freedom (Chicago: University of Chicago Press, 1962), p. 188: "A possible justification on liberal principles for compulsory purchase of annuities is that the improvident will not suffer the consequences of their own action but will impose costs on others. We shall not, it is said, be willing to see the indigent aged suffer in dire poverty. We shall assist them by private and public charity. Hence the man who does not provide for his old age will become a public charge. Compelling him to buy an annuity is justified not for his own good but for the good of the rest of us."

27   Milton Friedman, *Capitalism and Freedom* (Chicago: University of Chicago Press, 1962), p. 188.

28   For an explanation, see Anthony de Jasay, "Liberalism, Loose or Strict," *Independent Review*, v. IX, n. 3, Winter 2005, pp. 427-432.

29   F. A. Hayek, *The Constitution of Liberty* (Chicago: University of Chicago Press, 1960), p. 313.

The Paradox of Morality

30   Luckily the beggar was an outsider, for if he were from the Land of Gentlemen, the dispute would have continued indefinitely.

31   Lei Feng (December 18, 1940–August 15, 1962) was a soldier in the People's Liberation Army who became a national hero after his death in 1962 in a traffic accident. A national campaign to "Learn from Comrade Lei Feng" began in 1963; it called on the Chinese people to emulate his devotion to the Chinese Communist Party and to socialism.

32 "The Secret History of Self-Interest," in Stephen Holmes, *Passions and Constraints: On the Theory of Liberal Democracy* (Chicago: University of Chicago Press, 1995).

33 Quoted in Christine Caldwell Ames, *Righteous Persecution: Inquisition, Dominicans, and Christianity in the Middle Ages* (Philadelphia: University of Pennsylvania Press, 2008), p. 44.

34 Adam Smith, The Theory of Moral Sentiments, ed. D.D. Raphael and A.L. Macfie, vol. I of the Glasgow Edition of the Works and Correspondence of Adam Smith (Indianapolis: Liberty Fund, 1982). Chapter: a chap ii: Of the love of Praise, and of that of Praise–worthiness; and of the dread of Blame, and of that of Blame–worthiness; Accessed from http://oll.libertyfund.org/title/192/200125 on 2011-05-30.

35 Adam Smith, The Theory of Moral Sentiments, ed. D.D. Raphael and A.L. Macfie, vol. I of the Glasgow Edition of the Works and Correspondence of Adam Smith (Indianapolis: Liberty Fund, 1982). Chapter: b chap. i b: Of the beauty which the appearance of Utility bestows upon all the productions of art, and of the extensive influence of this species of Beauty; Accessed from http://oll.libertyfund.org/title/192/200137 on 2011-05-30.

36 Adam Smith, *An Inquiry Into the Nature and Causes of the Wealth of Nations*, Vol. 1 ed. R.H. Campbell and A.S. Skinner, vol. II of the Glasgow Edition of the Works and Correspondence of Adam Smith (Indianapolis: Liberty Fund: 1981). Chapter: [IV.ii] CHAPTER II: Of Restraints upon the Importation from Foreign Countries of such Goods as can be Produced at Home. Accessed from http://oll.libertyfund.org/title/220/217458/2313890 on 2010-08-23.

37 Smith, *An Inquiry Into the Nature and Causes of the Wealth of Nations*, Vol. 1 ed. R.H. Campbell and A.S. Skinner, vol. II of the Glasgow Edition of the Works and Correspondence of Adam Smith (Indianapolis: Liberty Fund: 1981). Chapter: [IV.viii] CHAPTER VIII: Conclusion of the Mercantile System. Accessed from http://oll.libertyfund.org/title/200/217484/2316261 on 2010-08-23.

38 "The specific characteristic of an economic relation is not its "egoism," but its "non-tuism." Philip H. Wicksteed, *The Commonsense of Political Economy, including a Study of the Human Basis of Economic Law* (London: Macmillan, 1910). Chapter: CHAPTER V: BUSINESS AND THE ECONOMIC NEXUS. Accessed from http://oll.libertyfund.org/title/1415/38938/104356 on 2010-08-23.

39 H.B. Acton, *The Morals of Markets and Related Essays,* ed. by David Gordon and Jeremy Shearmur (Indianapolis: Liberty Fund, 1993).

40 Voltaire, *Letters Concerning the English Nation,* ed. Nicholas Cronk (Oxford: Oxford University Press, 1999), p. 43.

The Market Economy and the Distribution of Wealth

41 The argument presented in what follows owes a good deal to ideas first set forth by Professor Mises in "Das festangelegte Kapital," in *Grundprobleme der Nationalökonomie*, pp. 201-14. [English trans. in *Epistemological Problems of Economics* (New York: D. Van Nostrand, 1960), pp. 217-31].

Human Betterment Through Globalization

42 The Foundation for Economic Education. www.fee.org.

Index of Proper Names
(Chinese names are listed by family name)

The Morality of Capitalism
Essay Contest

All students are invited to enter this companion essay contest! Submissions must be 500-750 words, and further instructions are available online.

1 Grand Prize: $1,000 + Scholarship to 2012 International Students For Liberty Conference

1 Second Place Prize: $200 + Scholarship to 2012 ISFLC

8 Runners Up: $100 each + Scholarship to 2012 ISFLC

Registration Deadline: December 1, 2011

Learn more at
www.StudentsForLiberty.org

Free Markets Need a Moral Defense: *Yours*

The Atlas Network has initiated a worldwide moral campaign for free enterprise, starting with honest debates about morality and capitalism in over a dozen languages. Atlas has partnered with the John Templeton Foundation's "Big Questions" program to promote serious discussion and debate about the morality of the free market and has partnered with Students For Liberty to bring you *The Morality of Capitalism*, a collection of essays edited by Atlas executive vice president Dr. Tom G. Palmer. Atlas is also sponsoring books, essay contests, and Freedom Schools on the morality of capitalism in over a dozen other languages, with the generous support of the Smith Family Foundation, the John Templeton Foundation, and other sponsors.

- The Atlas Network consists of over 400 independent, free-market think tanks and organizations that are based in the U.S. and in more than 80 countries.

- Atlas organizes training programs, regional conferences, and many other programs to identify and empower institutions and intellectual entrepreneurs who believe in liberty.

- If you'd like to become involved, visit AtlasNetwork.org and check out our worldwide directory, our "Think Tank Toolkit," and other online tools.

Your support can unlock the potential of free market capitalism to enrich the world, promote peace, and liberate the creative powers of the human mind. To sponsor a think tank or program, visit AtlasNetwork.org/donate.

ATLAS
NETWORK

202.449.8449 • 1201 L Street NW, Washington, DC 20005
AtlasNetwork.org

Empower Freedom Champions
Sponsor the Atlas Network!

Become an Atlas partner today, and help us train and empower the next generation of leaders who will protect and extend freedom. Liberty is too precious to let it wither or die. It needs our help. It needs your help.

AtlasNetwork.org/Donate

LE LIBERTY FUND

The Pierre F. and Enid Goodrich Foundation

The Pierre F. and Enid Goodrich Foundation (formerly Thirty Five Twenty, Inc.) is one of the philanthropic creations of Pierre F. Goodrich. Goodrich's major philanthropic interest was to create a lasting institutional legacy which would continue his lifelong promotion of the study of a society of free and responsible individuals. To this end Goodrich created Liberty Fund, Inc., in 1960, and endowed it with both financial assets and the guidance of the *Liberty Fund Basic Memorandum*. In 1996 Enid Goodrich made a further contribution to Liberty Fund, Inc.

The institutions and ideals of a free society that interested Goodrich were the rule of law; a market economy characterized by secure and transferable property rights; limited, constitutional government; political federalism; individual, personal responsibility over the conduct of one's life; and the duty of the individual to pursue a lifelong education into the nature of man, and his possibilities and imperfections.

Liberty Fund extends its educational activities, without cost to the public, through the following resources:

Online Library of Liberty
(oll.libertyfund.org)

This award-winning web site provides over 1,000 titles about individual liberty, limited government, and the free market. In addition to the classic books on liberty, there are educational aids and guides to help readers understand the texts.

Library of Economics and Liberty
(econlib.org)

This web site is dedicated to advancing the study of economics, markets, and liberty. It offers a unique combination of resources for students, teachers, researchers, and anyone interested in economics, including blogs and podcasts.

Liberty Fund, Inc.

8335 Allison Pointe Trail, Suite 300

Indianapolis, IN 46250.1684

Tel 317.842.0880

Toll Free 1.800.866.3520

Fax 317.577.9067

www.libertyfund.org

Students For Liberty

A Free Academy, A Free Society

Students For Liberty is a network of pro-liberty students all
over the world. We work to educate
our fellow students on the ideas of individual, economic, and
academic freedom.

Students For Liberty can help you with:

- Leadership training
- Tips on how to start a student group
- Finding speakers to host on campus
- Obtaining free books for a reading club
- Student Conferences

www.StudentsForLiberty.org

Students For Liberty Conferences

Do you want to:

- Learn about the philosophy of liberty?
- Meet fellow students and leaders of liberty?
- Receive training on how to best advance liberty?

Then join us for the

2011 Fall Regional Conferences

- Boston, MA
- New York City, NY
- Philadelphia, PA
- Winston-Salem, NC
- Chicago, IL
- Austin, TX
- Phoenix, AZ
- Pittsburgh, PA
- Los Angeles, CA
- San Francisco, CA

2012 International

Students For Liberty Conference

The world's largest gathering of pro-liberty students
February 17-19, 2012, in Washington DC.

www.PoliticalConferences.org

Additional Resources for Liberty

The Foundation
for Economic Education

– www.FEE.org –
– www.TheFreemanOnline.org –

The Cato Institute

– www.Cato.org –
– www.CatoOnCampus.org –

The Institute
for Humane Studies

– www.TheIHS.org –

The Foundation
for Individual Rights in Education

– www.TheFire.org –

The Charles G. Koch
Charitable Foundation

– www.CGKFoundation.org –

free enterprise

For Sir John Templeton, wealth creation was no accident of history, whether for the nations of the West or for the billions of people struggling for basic necessities in the developing world. Human societies could experience general prosperity, he believed, only when they recognized and established broad principles of freedom, competition, and personal responsibility. For him, individual freedom was the indispensable foundation of economic, social, and spiritual progress.

As one of the most successful investors of modern times, Sir John understood the enormous contribution that free markets and entrepreneurship could make to material improvement. As a student of classical liberalism, from Adam Smith to Milton Friedman, he also saw that, without economic freedom, individual freedom was fragile and vulnerable. The Foundation honors this profound vision by supporting a range of programs intended to liberate the initiative of individuals and nations and to establish the necessary conditions for the success of profit-making enterprise.

JOHN TEMPLETON FOUNDATION

SUPPORTING SCIENCE~INVESTING IN THE BIG QUESTIONS

www.templeton.org/ffe

"We need to change the narrative of capitalism, to show that it's about creating shared value, not for the few, but for everyone. If people could see that the way I see it, people would love capitalism the way I love it."
—John Mackey, CEO of Whole Foods Market

You Can Help Tell Young Americans About
The Morality of Capitalism

Capitalism today is "the greatest story never told" on far too many college campuses, in high schools, in the press, and by politicians seeking your votes by promising a bureaucratic administrative state will solve all the social and economic problems of "the economy"—problems that are almost always *caused* by politicians and bureaucrats.

Please consider giving copies of this book to students, teachers, the news media, local political, business and labor associations, and to your activist friends all across America! Knowledge is power in political debate. This book will give you that power.

Special Bulk Copy Discount Schedule

1 book $8.95	25 books $95.00	500 books $1,250.00
5 books $25.00	50 books $175.00	1000 books $2,000.00
10 books $45.00	100 books $325.00	

All prices include postage and handling.

JAMESON BOOKS, INC   **ORDER TOLL FREE**
P.O. Box 738   **800-426-1357**
Ottawa, IL 61350

Please send me _____ copies of *The Morality of Capitalism*.

I have enclosed my check for $ _____, or please charge my credit card:
    ☐ Visa   ☐ MasterCard

Card Number: _____ Exp Date: _____

Signature: _____

Name: _____

Address: _____

City: _____ State: _____ Zip code: _____

Illinois residents please add 6.5% sales tax. Please allow two weeks for delivery.